Praise for @MayorEmanuel

"Hilarious . . . The @MayorEmanuel account's profanity-laced tirades, one imagines, are what the real Emanuel would be saying if he could. It's Emanuel's imaginary internal monologue."
—Politico

"A hilariously dark journey of the soul in 140-character bursts. . . . It's hard not to feel like you've been on a journey with the man, even though the man has nothing to do with it."
—Chicago Tribune

"A hilarious send-up of the former White House chief of staff's campaign travails that comes complete with all the expletives in his arsenal."
—USA Today

"Go ahead and have a laugh at the foul-mouthed parody of Chicago's would-be mayor."
—The Huffington Post

"Angry, profane, and often surreal."
—New York Daily News

"Awesome."
—Village Voice

"Every so often, a work of art is created that is so new, so utterly at home in its medium, that you realized you've just witnessed a genuine cultural event. Such is the case with the saga of @MayorEmanuel, the brilliant—and completely fictional—Twitter account that led thousands of followers on a psychedelic, months-long journey through a parallel Chicago filled with rich allusions to the city, as well as innumerable other pieces of culture, both high and low."
—Wired

The
F***ing Epic
Twitter Quest of
@MayorEmanuel

Dan Sinker

Foreword by **Biz Stone**

SCRIBNER

New York   London   Toronto   Sydney   New Delhi

SCRIBNER
A Division of Simon & Schuster, Inc.
1230 Avenue of the Americas
New York, NY 10020

First Scribner trade paperback edition September 2011

SCRIBNER and design are registered trademarks of The Gale Group, Inc.,
used under license by Simon & Schuster, Inc., the publisher of this work.

For information about special discounts for bulk purchases,
please contact Simon & Schuster Special Sales at 1-866-506-1949
or business@simonandschuster.com.

The Simon & Schuster Speakers Bureau can bring authors to your live event.
For more information or to book an event contact the Simon & Schuster Speakers
Bureau at 1-866-248-3049 or visit our website at www.simonspeakers.com.

DESIGNED BY ERICH HOBBING

Manufactured in the United States of America

10 9 8 7 6 5 4 3 2 1

Library of Congress Control Number: 2011031169

ISBN: 978-1-4516-5514-8
ISBN: 978-1-4516-5518-6 (ebook)

For JD.

For ORD.

For KNTD.

Word is bond.

Under certain circumstances, profanity
provides a relief denied even to prayer.
—Mark Twain

Contents

Foreword

The Atlantic called it the "best fake Twitter account ever," and elevated @MayorEmanuel to a great cultural work by referring to it as an "epic poem." The *Chicago Tribune* declared it "a brilliantly imagined and unrestrained counter-script" to Rahm Emanuel's real-life, "polished and prim" mayoral campaign. *Esquire* celebrated the account as "screamingly funny, profane, and eventually poignant." Many have celebrated this groundbreaking literary achievement but ultimately the most important characterization comes down to one critical word—funny. Had this account not been funny, it very well may never have survived. More to the point, it might have been deleted.

Before cofounding Twitter, I worked at Google and, together with my colleague Jason Goldman, found myself in a heated debate with an executive legal team over the content policy for Blogger, the free, online, self-publishing platform we operated on Google's behalf. On most systems of this nature, impersonation is a breach of policy punishable by suspension or deletion of the account in question. At Google in 2003, there were many blogs that technically may have fallen under the category of impersonation, but they were obviously fake and often hilarious. These executives told us that we had to delete the accounts. Jason and I resisted: "No! They're funny!"

We insisted that solidly funny content should be allowed—especially if everybody knew it was just for laughs, because without humor, frankly, there is no point to life. The more we attempted to defend the issue in our jokey, irreverent manner, the deeper we dug ourselves into a hole with a bunch of guys in suits looking down at us wondering how in hell we ever managed to get a job at Google. A soft-spoken lawyer who wasn't wearing a suit and hadn't said much during the meeting finally piped up to explain that determining what is and what is not funny is too subjective. He nodded his head around the room and asked us if we wanted this team to design a test for funny content.

Our stunned faces answered "hell, no," but we kept quiet because it seemed like he wanted to help us. We were right to stay quiet because this guy went on to explain that in the case of a farcical impersonation, funniness was too subjective, but parody might be determined fairly by asking ourselves, "Would a reasonable person understand that this isn't real?" This approach took us out of the content mediation role and with that simple statement the argument was over. From that point on, impersonation would remain prohibited but parody would be permitted. That was a huge win for freedom of expression and helped pave the way for many more future policy wins.

I'm sharing a story that happened long before we founded Twitter because that soft-spoken Google lawyer is Alexander Macgillivray—Twitter's general counsel. On Twitter, our rules are clear. Impersonation is pretending to be another person or entity in order to deceive and may result in permanent account suspension, but parody is encouraged. We even suggest ways users can indicate that an account is not impersonation, such as a bio that distinguishes the account as parody. We think a reasonable person would understand that a man campaigning for political office would not use the following for his official bio: "Your next motherfucking mayor. Get used to it, assholes."

The free and open exchange of ideas and information can have life-changing impact. Humor is the most effective method we have to transmit information. Neurophysiology indicates that laughter is linked with the part of the brain that produces endorphins—natural hormonal stimulants that cause us to feel good. Not only that, but when we read something funny, we tend to share it with others so the information becomes a virus and spreads quickly from person to person. This is very likely why a simple parody limited to 140-character bursts became such a sensation. Science would suggest that simply by enjoying this collection of Tweets, you are significantly improving your health.

However, it is not only your health that the inimitable Dan Sinker has managed to improve in this now famous work. The very origins of parody are said to have come from Hegemon of Thasos, a Greek writer who took the wording of well-known poems, slightly altered them, and in so doing transformed the revered to the ridiculous. Here, Mr. Sinker has taken the modern micromedium of Twitter, and worked within the 140-character constraint to create an epic poem that simultaneously lampoons a political figure while celebrating the great city of Chicago. Each Tweet stands on its own, but in aggregate, an emergence takes place that is at once hilarious and sublime. To our health!

Biz Stone, Cofounder
Twitter, Inc.

The Epic

Rumors and Innuendo

Monday, September 27, 2010

fuck you right in your fucking face-hole. 09:52:09 PM

> And so it began, late in the evening, as news organizations started publishing rumors that Rahm Emanuel would be leaving his position as President Obama's chief of staff to throw his hat into the ring for Chicago's mayoral race. It would be the first competitive race in 21 years, following the announcement by mayor-for-life Richard M. Daley that he would not seek another four years in office.

Someone tell those fuckwads at @politico to shut their fucking trap, or I'll fucking END THEM. 10:11:12 PM

> Politico was the first to break the story, followed quickly by the rest of the political press.

Hey you douchebags at @ChicagoTribune, I'll fucking announce when I fucking announce. 10:22:18 PM

> This was the first, and only, @MayorEmanuel Tweet that I retweeted via @DanSinker. It made its way around Twitter pretty quickly, and @MayorEmanuel's follower count began to tick upwards rapidly.

Someone tell @joshtpm to shut his asshole before I have to hop an Acela Express and do it my goddamn self. 10:29:16 PM

> Josh Marshall at Talking Points Memo had picked up the Emanuel rumor story, as it quickly spread across the news.

If the Bears fuck this up, my entire platform is going to revolve around burning that stadium to the fucking ground. 10:34:24 PM

Goddamn right Bears win. 10:48:25 PM

The Chicago Bears beat their archrivals the Green Bay Packers 20–17. It's worth noting at this early point that I know nothing about sports. But if you're running for Mayor of Chicago, you'd better, so I followed the outcomes of all the Bears games on—where else—Twitter. Thank god this wasn't written in late spring, when I would have had to follow the outcomes of Cubs, Sox, Bulls, and Blackhawks games simultaneously.

Hey @jaketapper, you wanna talk "breaking," how about I break my foot off inside your colon? 10:58:01 PM

ABC News's Senior White House Correspondent Jake Tapper had just tweeted "BREAKING—Rahm Emanuel Likely to Leave White House This Week."

I swear to god, if I never have to see another cherry blossom as long as I goddamn live, it'll still be too fucking soon. 11:06:24 PM

Tuesday, September 28, 2010

Shit-screw you in your fucking cock-hole. 12:07:17 AM

Cocking shit-shiners it's late. 12:43:32 AM

And with that, day one ended. The follower count was around 500. Up from zero in three hours.

■ ■ ■

Gonna cram that sheriff's star so far up Dart's intestine that when he shits it'll look like the constellation Orion. 07:35:32 AM

Mayor Daley announced that he wouldn't run for reelection on September 7, 2010. By the 10th, news reports had Cook County Sheriff Tom Dart considering getting into the race. The Chicago *Sun-Times* quoted him as saying, "Voters know who I am; they appreciate a lot of the things we've done, so I think I do have the ability to have some 'head start' on some people." Prior to Emanuel announcing, Dart was at or near the top of polls.

Also, Sneed: stop talking about yourself in the third person or I swear to god, I will break my dick off and fuck you in the hair follicles. 07:37:46 AM

Michael Sneed is the leading political gossip reporter in Chicago. She writes about herself exclusively in the third person.

These people are fucking joking, right? Give me back my fucking house, or I will burn it down around you. 07:44:21 AM

When he left Congress to become Obama's chief of staff, the Emanuels (he is married with two children) rented their home in Chicago's Ravenswood neighborhood. That morning Sneed led with a report that the tenants in Emanuel's rental house were refusing to break their lease and allow Emanuel to move back into his home.

You know who I'm not going to miss at all? Mitch McConnell. That guy is the king of the fucking pansy-shitters. 07:50:48 AM

Mitch McConnell is the minority leader in the US Senate. He's the first of many Washington regulars that @MayorEmanuel realizes he'll soon be free of.

■ ■ ■

Some mornings coffee is like standing underneath a twat-rainbow while fucking a thousand puppies in the mouth. 08:22:32 AM

The first, and most graphic, of @MayorEmanuel's many coffee Tweets. Over the course of the feed, @MayorEmanuel would tweet about coffee another 69 times. Some of this was character logic: he's passionate about *everything*, so why not coffee too? Some of it was to help spread the account around Twitter: people would pass the coffee Tweets around rapid-fire. And part of it was that I really, really like coffee.

Jesus shit-Christ is it awkward around the office today. 09:24:03 AM

Wait a second: who the fuck holds a fucking election in Chicago in fucking FEBRUARY? 09:42:49 AM

We're all supposed to go out there with our dicks swinging in the snow? 09:45:54 AM

. . .

I will miss sneaking juice boxes with Sasha. 12:01:36 PM

I always liked the image of Emanuel and Sasha Obama sipping juice boxes in the White House Rose Garden.

. . .

Most of the lunch briefing was spent deciding whether I should drive down K Street yelling "Sayonara, bitches!" Or "Fuck you very much!" 02:21:05 PM

K Street is the epicenter for lobbyists and think tanks in Washington, DC.

Christ, the fuck train got derailed on its way to bullshit junction today. I blame Duncan. 02:43:54 PM

That'd be Arne Duncan, former CEO of the Chicago Public Schools, who was tapped to join Obama in Washington as the secretary of education. Fun fact: Duncan used to play professional basketball in Australia.

Another thing about Duncan: for being so tall, that guy is a fucking pussy when it comes to the head-fake. Makes him jump every goddamn time. 02:50:11 PM

When you're writing in 140 character bursts, visual gags work really well. The idea of @MayorEmanuel tossing out head-fakes was easy, visual shorthand for his aggressive personality.

. . .

Axelrod tells me "Who replaced Chicago with this shitfest?" isn't a good slogan. 03:32:45 PM

This was the first appearance of David Axelrod, who at the time was President Obama's chief strategist, having architected his campaign for president. Before entering the national spotlight with Obama's presidential campaign, Axelrod had been a longtime political strategist. Prior to entering politics, he was city hall reporter for the

Chicago Tribune in the early 1980s. He also sports a sweet Chicago-style mustache, which was the real motivating factor in incorporating him into the story. Axelrod was not actually directly involved in the Emanuel campaign in the way portrayed in the @MayorEmanuel story. He stayed in Washington, DC, though was seen in Chicago regularly during the mayoral race (and moved back in January 2011 to set up the Obama 2012 reelection headquarters in Chicago). His former political media firm AKP&D Message and Media (he's the "A," but he sold his interest when he joined the Obama administration) was paid millions by the Emanuel campaign to provide both media strategy and campaign consulting.

Wednesday, September 29, 2010

I really fucking hope that I get to stay on hold with Comcast Chicago all goddamn day. Yes, please, transfer me again. 09:31:31 AM

So Axelrod is blathering on about a "new Burnham plan" and I just look him square in the eye and say, "Fuck you, you fucking mustache-face." 10:02:20 AM

I'm not a motherfucking giant Snoopy balloon, so I will not appear at your motherfucking parade. 11:00:51 AM

This little trio of Tweets showed the challenges of moving back to Chicago and running for mayor beginning to come into focus for @MayorEmanuel: dealing with strategy sessions, being asked to appear at civic events, and hooking up utilities. All treated with equal amounts of disdain.

■ ■ ■

Geithner never stops talking. You can be standing there, double birds in his face and your cock hanging out, and he's all blah blah blah . . . 12:04:28 PM

Timothy Geithner is the US secretary of the Treasury.

I would rather lick the balls of the entire Chicago city counsel than have to deal with the fuck-nuggets in the House for another 10 minutes. 02:25:23 PM

DC, Comics

Thursday, September 30, 2010

Shitting cock-face, I stayed up way too late watching "Must Love Dogs" again. And I gotta deal with fucking Vilsack in the morning. **Fuck me.** 12:33:06 AM

> Tom Vilsack is the US secretary of agriculture.

■ ■ ■

Cock—06:36:17 AM

—a-doodle-doo, assholes. Wake the fuck up. 06:37:11 AM

■ ■ ■

If Dick Mell leaves another VM promising to be a "kingmaker," I'm going to pry all the keys off this phone and stuff them up his urethra. 08:13:03 AM

> Dick Mell is a longtime member of Chicago's city council. He was elected in 1975 and continues to serve on the council. Fun Fact: Mell's daughter Patricia is married to embattled former governor of Illinois Rod Blagojevich.

■ ■ ■

I walked into the briefing today, birds up, and said "Hey snatch-warblers, you've only got one day left with this bitch." It's official. 12:06:38 PM

> News reports had confirmed that Emanuel would be leaving the White House to run for mayor of Chicago. He'd be replaced by Pete Rouse, a senior advisor to the president and, up until news reports named him, someone whom many casual political observers had never heard of. I know I never had.

Jesus fuck-Christ, I told them that if they're going to go with Rouse, they'll have to find another billion in the budget for donut runs. 12:19:10 PM

Apparently they went with Rouse because the potted fucking bamboo in the fucking East Room was too busy. Too bad, the bamboo says more. 12:32:25 PM

Another thing about Rouse: hope you like your morning briefings around 11:45, because cock-asses that motherfucker can sleep in. 12:48:03 PM

■ ■ ■

Gibbs keeps looking at me and his eyes well up, like he's eating the dong-berries right off the pussy-bush. 02:15:30 PM

Robert Gibbs was the White House press secretary.

I would rather slam my dick in a door than look at the motherfucking yard sign samples Plouffe just e-mailed. 02:59:58 PM

David Plouffe, who was a chief campaign manager for Obama's election, appeared exclusively in this story in e-mails, faxes, and texts. This reflected the way many people experienced Plouffe: as a name in their in-box during the 2008 presidential campaign. Searching my Gmail, I had over 100 e-mails from Plouffe. In thinking about staffing up @MayorEmanuel's campaign, I decided that Plouffe would remain a virtual presence, just as he had for many of us in real life. To the best of my knowledge, Plouffe was not involved in the Emanuel campaign in real life, though he is the "P" in AKPD Message and Media, David Axelrod's consulting firm.

Salazar just came up with a fruit basket. Ken, unless you want me to insert these into your colon one-by-one, get the fuck out of my face. 04:58:37 PM

Ken Salazar is the US secretary of the interior.

■ ■ ■

Been eating Fiber One all day so I've got enough shit to go around tomorrow. Lieberman, be sure to check your mail: you just got shit-boxed. 07:52:26 PM

Joe Lieberman was a formerly Democratic senator from Connecticut who ran as an independent after losing the 2006 Democratic primary.

Last goddamn night in this fucking shit-coffin of a town. 10:19:44 PM

Friday, October 1, 2010

Thank god it's motherfucking shit-scratching cock-bleeding Friday.
07:40:47 AM

> This was it, the morning of Emanuel's departure from the White
> House. He met privately with the staff (where he was presented with
> a dead Asian carp wrapped in newspaper, echoing a mythic Emanuel
> moment, when he mailed a dead fish to a pollster who made him
> angry) and would then be publicly feted by the president himself. This
> was also the first of dozens of posts celebrating Friday—they would
> soon shift to end-of-work-week posts, usually tweeted right at 5:00.

**Dear Washington Press Corps, suck it out of my asshole, you
fucking third-rate, cock-handed, twat-cobbler hacks. I will miss
you not at all.** 08:58:44 AM

> "Suck it out of my asshole" was a nod to the Fake Steve Jobs character
> penned by tech journalist Dan Lyons—his character used the phrase
> so often he shortened it to "SIOOMA."

**Hey Steny Hoyer, check your mail today: You just got shit-boxed.
And I'm sure there's enough in there to pass around.** 09:04:13 AM

> Steny Hoyer was House majority leader from 2007 to 2011.

■ ■ ■

**LaHood just pulled up in his fucking electric clown car. This fucking
ceremony is going to last a dong-capping lifetime isn't it?** 09:15:12 AM

> Ray LaHood is the US secretary of transportation.

**Rouse just waddled up, panting like a leg-fucking schnauzer.
"Sorry I'm late." Yeah, you fuck-hat, I'm sure you are.** 09:32:43 AM

**Only thing getting me through this fucking thing is knowing my
shaking hand is covered in cock sweat.** 09:45:33 AM

**Vilsack's halitosis is like breathing through a scuba tank full of
dongs.** 10:01:05 AM

■ ■ ■

DCA > OR-MF-D. 10:37:31 AM

Presidential speech out of the way, Emanuel was off to Chicago.

Sweet Home

There is a pothole on the fucking Kennedy Expressway that I swear just made me cough up my sphincter. 03:47:15 PM

23 cock-socked, twat-fingered voicemails from Plouffe. In two hours! How many more before he figures out I'm not fucking answering? 04:26:44 PM

"Hey Rahm, David. I was thinking about strategies for the 32nd ward . . ." Fucking dick-trimming shit-sorcerers, I'm going to toss this phone. 04:32:18 PM

Home. I'm going to crack open this Half Acre tallboy, pop in Serendipity, and put my feet up. Fuck all of you in your cock-soaked armpits. 04:58:04 PM

Friday, October 1, 2010

Muff-shitting fuck-towers. 09:46:05 AM

It's @MayorEmanuel's first full day in Chicago, and many local political figures are stopping by his house, trying to catch a meeting. I have no idea if this is how the real Rahm's first day was, but I'm sure there were a lot of meetings over the first few days.

■ ■ ■

Thing I like about Quigley: that the dong-fountain calls me "sir." Thing I don't like: motherfucker thinks Saturday is a good day to drop by. 10:00:01 AM

Mike Quigley won Rahm Emanuel's vacated congressional seat in 2009.

I would rather snap a mousetrap inside my own asshole than take a meeting with Jody fucking Weis. 04:12:01 PM

> Jody Weis was the superintendent of police for Chicago.

The top-fucking fuck-topper: Burke. 05:21:31 PM

> Ed Burke is the longest continually serving alderman from a single ward in Chicago, having first been elected to office in 1969. He is the chair of the finance committee, and an extremely powerful and influential figure in the city council. But this was probably my least favorite Tweet of all of them. The concept was that Burke just shows up and @MayorEmanuel is immediately filled with dread, but it just didn't work—it fell flat. Capturing emotion in 140 characters was difficult at first.

Saturday, October 2, 2010

Axelrod has been standing outside my house in the rain all fucking day. Stopped knocking hours ago. What a shit-sad mustache he's got on. 08:18:12 PM

A cold, rainy October night? Someone tell Axelrod to pack his charts and head fucking home, I'm watching "1408." Boo, you fucking cock-tards. 09:05:37 PM

> Every film referenced to this point was a lesser-known film from John Cusack's catalog. This was a very early attempt at Chicago-related—Cusack grew up in the Chicago suburb of Evanston—character development.

Sunday, October 3, 2010

Holy fuck-smacks, where's the shit-coughing coffee? 08:33:44 AM

■ ■ ■

183 e-mails from Plouffe later, and the suck-fucking webtards still made a site that looks like Barack's. 01:30:32 PM

> Emanuel's campaign website, chicagoforrahm.com, debuted and its color scheme and font choice made it look very similar to the Obama 2008 campaign site.

Axelrod's shooting my "special video announcement" (WTF?) for tomorrow. Wants me to say "Daley's stewardship" and I keep saying "sewer-shit." 01:47:54 PM

If Axelrod says ". . . and action!" one more time like he's Martin fucking Scorsese I'm going to cram his Flipcam into his fucking colon. 02:43:55 PM

■ ■ ■

If Axelrod doesn't get back here with a Home Run Inn deep dish before the game starts, I'm going to dunk his fucking head in the fuck-tank. 06:36:59 PM

> I received approximately two dozen Tweets in response to this one, pointing out that the Home Run Inn, a longtime Chicago pizza place on Chicago's Southwest Side, doesn't actually serve deep dish. Totally caught doing shitty research, the only reply I could come up with was "maybe not for YOU."

Solis just stopped by and was all, "Oh, you guys are watching the game?" Now I'm chucking my chicken wing gristle at his huge fucking head. 08:25:29 PM

> Danny Solis is an alderman in Chicago, and the head of the zoning commission.

Jesus fucking Christ-on-a-Cock, could this Bears game be any more fucking boring? Helen Shiller plays better motherfucking ball than this. 09:00:37 PM

> Helen Shiller is one of the more vocal left-leaning aldermen in Chicago.

Plouffe e-mailed to say that even if my listening tour tomorrow is spent listening to cock-bulbs complain about this game, I still have to go. 09:19:03 PM

Fucking dong-choke, if I was invited to a zoning board meeting right now I'd go in a heartbeat—has to be more exciting than this game. 09:26:03 PM

Fuck this game right in its fucking shit-sack. Axelrod had the right idea: He fell asleep in the middle of the first quarter. 10:32:43 PM

The Bears lost to the New York Giants 17–4 in a game that the *Chicagoist* called "the ugliest game we've ever seen."

Listening Tour

Monday, October 4, 2010

I'm going to have to drink an entire fucking bottle of Purell when I get home from all this shit-blasting hand-shaking. 10:33:41 AM

This was the first day of Emanuel's "Tell It Like It Is" tour of Chicago. Even though he was sent off from Washington in style—a hug from the president, even—he didn't actually announce that he was running for mayor. This listening tour was the first event in a very orchestrated run-up to an official announcement.

■ ■ ■

Jesus shit-painting nut-Christ, February is way fucking far away. 04:08:05 PM

What I learned on today's listening tour: You know what's wrong with Chicago? Every fucking motherfucking thing. 04:32:28 PM

■ ■ ■

After consulting with this four-pack of Gossamer Ale, it's decided: Axelrod's mustache can do the fucking listening tour on its own tomorrow. 07:39:42 PM

Gossamer Ale is brewed by local Chicago craft brewers Half Acre. It is delicious.

Frick-fucking crimp-cramming dick-jammers. 08:26:45 PM

Tuesday, October 5, 2010

Jesus fuck-chomping Christ, everything's shit-shape today. 08:32:32 AM

Text from Plouffe: "Try to grimace less when shaking hands." One of these days I'm going to give that motherfucker a reason to grimace. 08:47:01 AM

Who the fuck is in charge of cleaning the CTA stations? Because at this point I wouldn't mind taking a fucking meeting with that asshole. 09:18:37 AM

The actual Rahm Emanuel visited every single CTA L station (the L is the public train system in Chicago, so named because much of the line is elevated aboveground) during his campaign, many of them multiple times. Most of them are not very clean.

■ ■ ■

Shitting-fuck-sausage. How do you fucking people eat like this? 11:58:00 AM

The early days of Emanuel's listening tour seemed to be exclusively focused on public transportation and lunch places.

Please, fucking pretty please with fucking sugar on top, stuff your camera into my face again, you fucking snatch-hole. 01:28:15 PM

■ ■ ■

Just fucking perfect: Axelrod's Civic just broke down in Chinatown. Again. Cock-stump. 02:21:26 PM

This was the first appearance of Axelrod's trusty 1994 Honda Civic. I have no idea what kind of car the real David Axelrod drives, or ever drove, but I owned a white '94 Civic for years. This fictional car was based on that real one.

Manny Flores just drove by and chucked a can at me while Axelrod's trying to change this tire. Fucking. Worst. Fucking. Day. Fucking. Ever. 03:10:45 PM

Manny Flores is a former alderman who now serves as the director of the Illinois Department of Financial and Professional Regulation. He was another early name in the mayoral race, going so far as to collect signatures for the ballot.

Christ, when this day is over, I'm going to devour an entire Eli's fucking cheesecake like I'm a motherfucking Cathy cartoon. Ack! 03:32:5

> When the Emanuel campaign released its campaign finance records in January, it turned out they'd spent almost $15,000 on Eli's Cheesecake.

■ ■ ■

Shrimp-sock fish-cock. I'm done with this fucking day. 08:12:30 PM

Talk to the Cock

Wednesday, October 6, 2010

Whichever one of you motherfuckers got me sick, you can go vote for Rickey fucking Hendon. To the rest of you—who's got some fucking soup? 07:10:01 AM

> Former State Senator Rickey Hendon was another early name in the mayoral race. Hendon, a longtime presence in the local and state political scene, resigned his seat in February 2011. On a national level, he's probably best known for getting into an argument about a vote with Barack Obama, when they both were state senators, that reportedly ended with Obama having "to be physically restrained."

■ ■ ■

Sick, wearing nothing but a fucking bathrobe, going to meet with the Tribune Editorial Board. "That's their dress code," e-mails Plouffe. 10:10:17 AM

> The same day that Emanuel was scheduled to meet with the influential paper's editorial board, the *New York Times* dropped a major story about the Tribune Company, "At Flagging Tribune, Tales of a Bankrupt Culture." It was a greatest-hits collection of sordid stories from the Tribune Tower, many circulating around the boorish behavior of then-Tribune company CEO Randy Michaels.

Apparently it's just me and Randy Michaels in bathrobes at the Tribune Tower. The king of the fucking ass-clowns. Great. Thanks, Plouffe. 11:25:48 AM

Michaels keeps interrupting the board's questions by standing up, opening his bathrobe and yelling "TALK TO THE COCK!!" Fucking fuck fuckers. 12:34:47 PM

I would rather punch myself in the cock every hour on the hour than have to sit through something that humiliating again. Fucktard Tower. 02:53:57 PM

Fucking fuck-shitting motherfucking shit-fuck motherfuckers. 03:17:34 PM

■ ■ ■

Yes, alderman, I am fucking delighted to have dinner at Harold's Chicken Shack. These motherfucking arteries aren't going to clog themselves. 05:54:01 PM

Waguespack keeps jogging by my house. Little short-shorts. I'm just standing in the front yard, birds up, waiting for the motherfucker. 07:49:31 PM

> Alderman Scott Waguespack was another early contender in the mayoral race. In all, Progress Illinois, which tracked early movement in the race, had more than 40 names on its list of potential candidates.

And there he fucking goes a-fucking-gain: jog-jog-jog. WHAT THE FUCK?! 07:56:15 PM

I'm going to go for a jog up Waguespack's motherfucking colon if he comes back around again. 08:03:52 PM

■ ■ ■

Fuck it. I'm fucking sick. I'm fucking tired. It's a fucking "America's Sweethearts" kind of night. 09:59:54 PM

Fucking Fund-raising

Thursday, October 7, 2010

Tick-tock, shit-cocks. Time to wake up. 07:28:54 AM

Dow over 11,000 on the same day I'm going on a listening tour of Penny Pritzker's pocketbook? Eyes on the sky for a twat-rainbow. Trifecta! 08:02:21 AM

> Chicago billionaire Penny Pritzker is the most visible member of the Pritzker family, one of the richest families in America. It seems like almost everything in Chicago, from the bandshell in Millennium Park to a public school to a military museum, is named after the Pritzkers. Penny donates a lot of time and money to political candidates, including her own former service as the finance chair of Obama's presidential campaign (and she was at one point considered to be a top contender for commerce secretary). She also serves on a number of high-profile nonprofit boards in Chicago and, after Emanuel was elected mayor, was appointed to the Chicago Board of Education.

Penny keeps a money room in her house, and dives into it like she's Scrooge McDuck. We've been swimming in it all morning. Fucking glorious. 11:19:38 AM

Nothing like a money-swim to get a guy feeling in cock-shape again. Axelrod, pull your Civic around: I've got some fucking hands to shake. 12:11:04 PM

Just got cut off on West Madison by a fucking cupcake truck. Eighth one I've seen. The fuck is up with you and cupcakes you fucking fatties? 12:30:40 PM

OK, West Garfield Park, come get your hand shaken. I promise when elected you'll see me less than you see the inside of a unicorn's vagina. 01:10:34 PM

• • •

Dinner with Obama at Alexi fundraiser. Fucking Alexi—getting caught chatting with him is like being sucked into a black hole of cocks. 04:05:56 PM

That's Alexi Giannoulias, Democratic candidate for Senate, who was running to fill Barack Obama's old seat, a seat the GOP desperately wanted to win. Giannoulias, the candidate Democrats chose to defend it, found himself embroiled in controversy surrounding his family's failed bank (it was shut down by the FDIC two weeks after Giannoulias won the Democratic primary). In a year in which the economy and federal bank bailout played heavily in the election, it wasn't a great situation to be in.

If Obama doesn't show soon, I'm out. Have been stuck inside the Giannoulias dong-vortex for a motherfucking hour now. 05:34:28 PM

Emanuel was actually not at the Giannoulias fund-raiser. In fact, according to ABC 7, "Emanuel was told to keep a low profile so as not to upstage the president and Alexi Giannoulias."

Alexi is "entertaining" the guests by seeing how many dinner rolls he can stuff in his fucking mouth. He's up to seventeen. 05:59:01 PM

■ ■ ■

Jesus Christ-on-a-fuck, that's four hours of my life I'm never going to get back. Alexi is as dumb as the fucking day is fucking long. 07:42:27 PM

By the way, the final motherfucking bread-roll count? Thirty-fucking-two. In at once. Mama Regenstein vomited into the salad plate. 07:51:16 PM

The Regensteins, like the Pritzkers, are another hyper-wealthy Chicago family. They even have an ape house named after them. I have no idea who "Mama" Regenstein is.

Fucking cock-sanding shit-branding, I am tired. 10:22:57 PM

Public Servant

Friday, October 8, 2010

Good motherfucking morning, motherfuckers. 07:01:29 AM

Strategy session. Axelrod thinks "I want to be like motherfucking Rahm" is a bad campaign slogan. The fuck? It worked for Jordan. 08:49:21 AM

> Bulls legend Michael Jordan was featured in a series of Gatorade commercials in the 1990s where kids proclaimed they wanted to "be like Mike."

Axelrod also dismissed Ari's idea of a movie where politicians team up with cartoon characters to fight an intergalactic menace. Fuck fuck. 09:09:02 AM

> The 1996 film *Space Jam* featured Michael Jordan and the Looney Toons. IMDb spells out the plot succinctly: "Michael Jordan agrees to help the Looney Toons play a basketball game vs. alien slavers to determine their freedom." So there's that.

Axelrod says no way: "Remember when the Bulls won for the sixth time and it felt like getting fucked on a pile of ponies? Vote Rahm." 09:20:47 AM

■ ■ ■

How did you know that listening to you bitch was exactly what I wanted to do on a beautiful fucking Friday? 03:47:30 PM

> The listening tour continued.

Why is it the only fucking places I find you people are riding the L or stuffing your fucking face? Or, worse, both? 03:51:54 PM

I will tell you this though: stand on a fucking L platform long enough and you will see every shade of vomit known to man. Vibrant! 04:04:05 PM

■ ■ ■

I just became the mayor of Fuck You in the Fucking Face, it's Friday on @foursquare. 04:13:40 PM

Axelrod's on his way over with a bucket of chicken, a growler of Half Acre and his copy of "2012." TGIMFF. 06:24:11 PM

Saturday, October 9, 2010

Plouffe just faxed over the itinerary. I've got to hit 13 farmer's markets. Here's a secret: edible greens scare the shit out of me. **Fuck.** 08:47:35 AM

■ ■ ■

Jesus motherfucking Christ, I hope to never see another winter squash in my motherfucking life. Fuck you and your fucking farmer's markets. 05:20:29 PM

Also, Chicago, what the fuck is up with all the baby strollers? Did you spend the two goddamn years I was gone just fucking non-stop? 06:11:24 PM

Long-Distance Runner

Sunday, October 10, 2010

Christ, I'm going to have to shake a lot of fucking sweaty hands today, aren't I? First sign of bloody nipples and I'm fucking GONE. 08:47:30 AM

> The first Chicago Marathon was run on Saturday, September 23, 1905, less than a decade after the first Olympic marathon. Some 38,132 runners ran in the 2010 race.

I know I'm supposed to say you're all heroic athletes, but I just saw a guy in a chicken suit puke up a Clif Bar at mile fucking three. 09:15:19 AM

■ ■ ■

Congratulations, marathon runners! You're 26.2 miles closer to a motherfucking knee replacement! 05:19:23 PM

Axelrod's mustache finished the cock-shocking marathon in 5:38. 07:18:18 PM

■ ■ ■

Just looked over Plouffe's itinerary for the week. It is fucktacularly stupid. How long does this goddamn listening tour have to last again? 09:23:28 PM

Talk to the Disembodied Hand

Monday, October 11, 2010

So which godforsaken corner of this motherfucking city am I headed to today in this never-ending dick-slamming tour? 08:14:35 AM

I refuse to choke down another fucking pepper and egg sandwich. Seriously, how has this entire city not died from a coronary? 09:26:29 AM

> The pepper-and-egg is a uniquely Chicagoan breakfast: it's scrambled eggs and green peppers stuffed inside a toasted French bread roll. Mozzarella cheese is optional. Local history assigns the invention of the pepper-and-egg sandwich to the influx of Catholic immigrants from Italy looking for a meal to replace meat on Fridays during Lent. Like many Chicago culinary delights, it is incredibly delicious. And it will kill you dead one day.

Dick Mell is the king of the pepper and egg. Eats three or four of them every morning. Ends up smelling like a sulfur bath all day. 09:33:14 AM

■ ■ ■

Seriously considering having my shaking hand amputated and sending it around the city alone so I can get some actual fucking work done. 05:38:33 PM

Hey, Sauganash, come shake the disembodied hand of Rahm Emanuel tomorrow, while I'm busy not giving a fuck about you somewhere else. 05:43:42 PM

> Sauganash is a neighborhood on the far northwest side of the city.

Fucking seriously, doesn't Flores have any "listening" to do? Come on: Carol Moseley Braun doesn't have to "listen" to any motherfuckers? 06:02:54 PM

That would be one-term Senator Carol Moseley Braun, the first (and only) African-American woman elected to the US Senate. Elected to the Senate in 1992, she served as ambassador to New Zealand after she lost reelection, and briefly ran for the Democratic nomination for president in 2004. Since then, she's maintained a low profile, running a small coffee and tea import business in Chicago called Ambassador Organics. Her entrance into the mayoral race, which happened before Emanuel's, took many by surprise, as she'd effectively been out of local politics since her Senate win.

Yet here I am fucking "listening" to all you fucking v-holes prattle on and on about fucking potholes and parking meters every fucking day. 06:05:04 PM

New slogan: "Hey Chicago: Just park in the fucking space and be done with it. Emanuel '11." 06:09:17 PM

Mayor Daley leased the rights to the parking meters in a spectacularly awful 75-year deal worth $1.16 billion. While the sketchy specifics of the actual deal were reported widely after the fact, what most people were up in arms about was the fact that it replaced meters with pay boxes, and you'd have to walk an entire half-block to pay. People were really pissed about that.

Scowling through the Columbus Day Parade, Ed Burke said I had a case of the Mondays. More like the Can't-Fucking-Stand-You Days. 08:59:28 PM

Tuesday, October 12, 2010

Someone fucking needs to fucking bring me a fucking coffee this very fucking second. 08:12:56 AM

■ ■ ■

Jesus fucking cock-twats: Biden is in town? Fucking Christ, I'll be hiding out in a goddamn undisclosed location for the rest of the day. 12:59:35 PM

Vice President Joe Biden came to Chicago to stump for Illinois Governor Pat Quinn, who took over as governor when Rod Blagojevich was arrested for attempting to sell Barack Obama's former Senate seat. Quinn was running for his first elected term as governor.

■ ■ ■

Would someone fucking pledge to WBEZ already so those sad fucking radio-tards will shut the fuck up? 05:10:32 PM

WBEZ is the major public radio station in Chicago.

The "Stuck in a Mine" Strategy

Fuck yes, you Chilean miner sons-of-bitches, fuck yes. 11:00:01 PM

News had just broken that 33 Chilean miners, stuck in a collapsed gold and copper mine for 69 days, were about to be rescued.

Wednesday, October 13, 2010

New slogan: "Because Chicago is in a deeper fucking hole than the fucking Chilean miners. Vote Rahm." 08:49:19 AM

I've got Axelrod looking into where to get one of those miner rescue elevators so I can ride one around Ed Burke's lower fucking intestine. 08:55:23 AM

If you need me today, I'll be at home watching CNN and bawling like a motherfucking baby. 09:35:22 AM

■ ■ ■

Been on BBM with Plouffe, selling him on my "stuck in a mine" strategy. (1) don't have to shake fucking hands; (2) in 90 days you'll love me. 05:01:22 PM

Axelrod just came over and we're both wearing hard hats and only eating food we can cram through a motherfucking 6" hole. This is the life. 05:41:28 PM

You would be amazed just how many different kinds of food you can stuff through a 6" hole. Axelrod got an entire fucking turkey through. 07:58:27 PM

I find the Chilean miner rescue incredibly moving. Once this last guy is up, we're going to send 'em all back down, right? Fuck yes. 08:00:54 PM

■ ■ ■

So everyone's up from the mine? Jesus fucking Christ-twat . . . now what? 10:25:59 PM

> Every miner was brought up, one at a time, from the mine in a 21"-diameter capsule, a ride that took 15 minutes.

Thursday, October 14, 2010

I woke up with a hard hat in my hands, looked up at the hole Axelrod and I drilled in the ceiling, and just started fucking weeping. Emptiness. 07:34:50 AM

I know it's not reasonable but, deep fucking down, I bet you too wish they'd continue to pull Chileans up from the ground forever. 07:36:51 AM

What has brought this city closer together than feeling motherfucking one with 33 people stuck in the ground of another continent? Nothing. 07:41:46 AM

New slogan: "Bring back that first miner feeling. Emanuel for motherfucking mayor." 07:45:33 AM

A Field of Dong-Tards and Shit-Eaters

I actually wanted Madigan to run. Have you seen the rest of the shit-tards that have announced? Give me someone fucking competent. 12:42:33 PM

> Lisa Madigan, the attorney general for Illinois and daughter of the power broker of the statehouse, Speaker of the House Mike Madigan,

was another name high on the list of possible mayoral contenders. While there was a great deal of media attention and public support for the idea of her entering the race, she officially announced on Chicago Public Radio that she was out.

Is it too late to get in on the fucking attorney general race? Come on, Madigan, let's do this! Don't leave me with Hendon and Flores. 03:33:50 PM

Flores had actually dropped out of the race four days before, a fact that I'd completely missed.

Unless motherfucking Oprah motherfucking Winfrey enters this race, it's going to be me against a field of dong-tards and shit-eaters. 03:38:09 PM

Seriously, a debate with these shit-galoids will end with me crushing my cock with the podium, just to feel SOMETHING. 03:43:31 PM

New slogan: "Vote Rahm: Because Jesus cock-Christ, look at the other fucking guys." 03:58:10 PM

If I'd have known the field was going to end up this fucking limp-dicked, I'd have stayed in Washington through the fucking midterms. 04:10:46 PM

Enter the Intern

Friday, October 15, 2010

Right about now I'm getting that sinking fucking feeling that I was served motherfucking decaf. 08:40:10 AM

■ ■ ■

Fucking Friday night fucking starts fucking right fucking now. 04:02:17 PM

So the e-mail started "Dear First Name." That was Plouffe's quick fix to the original: "Dear Motherfucking Twat-tards." 05:20:48 PM

The early days of the real Emanuel campaign were not the smoothest. Their first e-mail blast, sent Friday afternoon, was addressed to "Dear First Name."

Dear First Name, Fuck you in your fucking pie-hole, you stupid motherfucking snatch-drip. Yours, Rahm. 05:27:52 PM

Dear First Name, Who's got one and a half middle fingers, six beers, and doesn't give a fuck if I got your name right? This guy. 05:34:08 PM

I have no idea if the real Rahm Emanuel is a heavy drinker, but @MayorEmanuel sure was.

Dear First Name, Plouffe assures me that we're going to have an actual fucking communications team in place soon. The intern is a cocktard. 05:40:25 PM

"The intern is a cocktard" was the first mention of a soon-to-be central character in this story, invented entirely thanks to the Dear First Name e-mail.

Saturday, October 16, 2010

Holy shit-cocks, I should have stopped at nine beers last night. My fucking head is going to fucking explode at this breakfast meeting. 08:39:00 AM

Of course Axelrod waltzes into the meeting like he drank nothing last night. That motherfucker's liver is made of motherfucking Teflon. 11:03:50 AM

■ ■ ■

Fucking shine on, you motherfucking amazing fucking sun. 01:05:09 PM

Shitwork

Sunday, October 17, 2010

Fuck your motherfucking Sunday morning, I'm sleeping until goddamn noon. 08:59:21 AM

■ ■ ■

Fucking motherfucking fuck-shitting ass-cocked Bears. 02:47:05 PM

The Bears lost to the Seattle Seahawks, 23–20.

■ ■ ■

I really did try to listen to that fucking debate. But as soon as Quinn opens his mouth, I feel like a little part of me cock-plucking dies. 10:31:29

The aforementioned Pat Quinn was running for his first elected term as governor.

Monday, October 18, 2010

Shit-shaking dong-stompers. 08:27:47 AM

Really, what's a few motherfucking million raised? Don't fucking worry, Dart, I'm sure someone will give you some cash at some point. 03:47:09 PM

Rumors were beginning to circulate in the press that Emanuel had already raised millions—even before officially declaring that he was a candidate for mayor. His fund-raising prowess significantly complicated the life of anyone attempting to run against him.

■ ■ ■

Today was one never-ending fucking strategy session. Workloads doubled when Axelrod's mustache announced it was taking the week off. 08:46:48 PM

Seriously, if that motherfucking 'stache is talking to fucking Meeks, I'm going to lose it. 08:48:20 PM

That'd be James Meeks, a mayoral candidate, Illinois state senator and pastor of the 24,000-member Salem Baptist Church in Chicago's Pullman neighborhood on the far South Side. To the best of my knowledge, he never had a meeting with David Axelrod's mustache.

Axelrod says it's just taking a few days to see the fall colors in WI, but really: what fucking mustache takes off two weeks before midterms? 08:50:53 PM

Anyway, a week without that mustache just went from a slog to a motherfucking full-fledged shit-wallow. 08:54:38 PM

Tuesday, October 19, 2010

I'm going to close my eyes and imagine a coffeepot as big as the motherfucking Sears motherfucking Tower. 08:00:16 AM

> Chicago's Sears Tower, the tallest building in America (and at one point, the world), was renamed the Willis Tower in 2009 when a London-based insurance broker took over three of the building's 110 floors. Everyone still calls it the Sears Tower, except apparently a handful of assholes on Twitter, who have to point out that it's *actually* called the Willis Tower now. It's fun to fuck with them.

■ ■ ■

You want to know my definition of hell? This motherfucking lunch meeting that the fucking communications intern set up with Billy Dec. Fuck. 12:04:33 PM

> For all the aldermen, cabinet secretaries, and other little-known names that are dropped in this story, the littlest known has to be Billy Dec. A club owner in Chicago, he briefly entered Chicago political consciousness in the lead-up to Chicago's failed bid for the 2016 Olympics, when he posted YouTube videos of himself with various celebrities, asking them how they felt about the Olympics coming to Chicago.

Jesus fucking Christ, apparently it's take-a-lunch-meeting-with-a-raging-douchebag day. 12:09:22 PM

Fuck me. He's wearing his "dressy" baseball hat. Asked Axelrod to circle the block one more time. Considering jumping into traffic. 12:17:06 PM

That was a half hour I'll never fucking get back. On the upside, the Rumble in the Jungle Turkey Wrap at the Rainforest Cafe—tasty! 12:43:10 PM

Next time I even hear the motherfucking name Billy Dec, I'm slamming my cock in the door of Axelrod's Civic. 02:41:31 PM

■ ■ ■

Watching Alexi and Kirk debate is like fucking a sackful of dumb.
07:36:52 PM

Alexi Giannoulias's opponent was Republican Mark Kirk.

Wednesday, October 20, 2010

Going around the public schools with Huberman today. That guy smells like motherfucking sadness. 08:04:29 AM

While Emanuel did tour public schools that week, he didn't do it with Ron Huberman. Huberman was the CEO of the Chicago Public Schools, having taken over the position after Arne Duncan moved to Washington, DC. He would resign his position on November 29, 2010.

Axelrod tells me it's not a word but Jesus fucking Christ it's going to take a bazillion fucking dollars to save these fucking schools.
02:36:15 PM

In fact, the Chicago Public Schools face a deficit of around $750 million.

Thursday, October 21, 2010

I've asked Axelrod to come over and just pour the coffee straight into my mouth while I'm still lying here. "I'll be right over!" 07:12:10 AM

Christ, I'm so fucking tired I forgot to swear in that last Tweet: fucking motherfucking shit cock ass fuck twat. Feeling better already. 07:33:11 AM

So Ari is throwing me a fund-raiser soon, except he keeps calling it a "fuck-raiser." I don't even know what that fucking means. He scares me. 07:40:46 AM

Ari is, of course, Ari Emanuel, Rahm's younger brother and a major power player in the entertainment industry. He's the inspiration for the Ari Gold character in the TV show *Entourage*. If you've seen the show, that means you now know more about Ari Emanuel than I do. The press reported that Ari would throw a fund-raiser for Emanuel in LA on November 4.

But, I'd rather be on a flight to LA than have to tour another pathetic fucking school. Today's might as well be the Oliver Twist Academy. 07:54:14 AM

Sufficiently coffeed. Alright, Chicago, I'm going to fuck you in the fucking face today. 08:28:08 AM

Dart Rules!

If Dart's rent-a-cops pull over Axelrod's Civic one more time, I'm going to stuff my fist so far up his ass my stump will tickle his uvula. 03:36:22 PM

Axelrod just called me from the impound. Dart's goons hauled his fucking Civic in. Oh, it's motherfucking on now, you fucking motherfuck. 05:50:53 PM

Sheriff Woody from "Toy Story" is more of a real lawman than that cocktard Dart. "There's a motherfucking snake in my boot." 06:05:43 PM

Friday, October 22, 2010

Axelrod just pulled up in his Civic, gave a beep and I went out. The thing has DART RULES spraypainted across the motherfucking hood. 07:24:15 AM

■ ■ ■

I'm going to have to drink ten thousand motherfucking beers to make this day motherfucking better. 04:06:23 PM

Chicago, it's really fucking easy: Put down the fucking mouse, walk out the fucking door, it's fucking Friday. 04:34:00 PM

Axelrod just showed up with a fucking case of toilet paper. We're going to TP the living shit out of Dart's house! 06:50:41 PM

Saturday, October 23, 2010

If you think I'm getting out of fucking bed on a rainy Saturday, you're out of your motherfucking cock-holed mind. 12:09:17 PM

The fuck is Plouffe sending me to store openings for? What's next, being a motherfucking greeter at the Pullman Walmart? 01:43:44 PM

> Emanuel made an appearance at the blocks-long lineup for the grand opening of the Apple Store in Chicago's wealthy Lincoln Park neighborhood. The Walmart in Pullman (the first to open in Chicago) will open in 2013—I would expect that Emanuel will in fact be there.

And seriously, there is an entirely different class of douchebag that shows up at an Apple Store opening in Lincoln fucking Park. 01:47:55 PM

Who wants a MacBook Air with a side of asshole? Order fucking up. 01:55:14 PM

■ ■ ■

Fucking Christ, morning at the Apple Store, afternoon at Whole Foods. Suck it out of my asshole, Lincoln Park! 07:16:54 PM

Sunday, October 24, 2010

Hey, Chicago, get your hands off your fucking cock and get the fuck outside. It's motherfucking incredible out here. 01:00:28 PM

■ ■ ■

I swear to fucking god, Honeycrisp apples are motherfucking twat-licious! 03:17:38 PM

Cameos too—you put that shit into your fucking face-hole and you think, "Motherfucker, I am eating a fucking apple." 03:31:33 PM

Monday, October 25, 2010

Fuck your fucking Monday morning right in its fucking puckered fucking pink fucking asshole. 07:26:36 AM

Axelrod's mustache was back today after its week off. Good to have that bushy motherfucker back. 06:37:49 PM

■ ■ ■

Batten down the hatches, motherfuckers! 08:19:10 PM

The news had been filled with warnings about a coming windstorm—
2,200 miles long, with hurricane-speed winds.

**Axelrod's refusing to come up from the basement. Pretty sure
that motherfucker's eaten most of the canned peaches. Fuck me.**
08:28:49 PM

**Axelrod's calling up from the basement, telling me I shouldn't
be up on the roof yelling, "BRING IT ON, YOU WINDY
MOTHERFUCKERS."** 10:34:05 PM

Tuesday, October 26, 2010

**COME ON YOU FUCKING WEATHER, IS THIS THE BEST YOU
FUCKING GOT?** 07:49:06 AM

**Now there's motherfucking blue motherfucking skies out there.
This goddamn wind storm can fucking blow me.** 10:23:52 AM

In Chicago, the much-hyped windstorm didn't amount to much. The
Chicago Tribune reported that, "It was hard for some in the city—
where the weather was cloudy and blustery—to reconcile what they
saw with descriptions of this being 'the largest storm in decades.'" That
would be because it wasn't.

Wednesday, October 27, 2010

C-fuck-O-fuck-F-fuck-F-fuck-E-fuck-E. 07:13:21 AM

So I see that motherfucker Dart got that shit-box I sent him.
10:49:24 AM

Hey, Chicago, meet the new motherfucking sheriff in town.
10:51:25 AM

Tom Dart announced that he would not seek the office of mayor,
citing the impact it would have on his family. He remains the sheriff
of Cook County.

A Field of Fucking Pussies

Strategy session: do we just hold the fucking election early? Or do we not fucking bother at all? Seems like a fucking formality now. 10:54:34 AM

Axelrod's telling me I need to do more at this news conference than let them film my motherfucking victory lap. 12:47:50 PM

■ ■ ■

Dear Chicago, I'm sorry that 21 years of Daley gave you a field of fucking pussies. And me. 06:18:12 PM

But really, when I look at this fucking pathetic field and the most credible candidate casts dicks in cement, I mostly feel sorry for you. 06:31:31 PM

> So in an election that was not wanting for characters, an early candidate was Cynthia Albritton, better known as Cynthia Plaster Caster, an artist who made a name for herself casting the penises of musicians. For real. The song "Plaster Caster," by Kiss? That's about her. She dubbed her political party "The Hard Party" and distributed pins urging voters to "Erect Cynthia Plaster Caster for Mayor." Unfortunately, she never turned in signatures to officially get on the ballot.

New slogan: "I mostly feel sorry for you, you pathetic fucking shit-tards. Emanuel '11." 06:41:02 PM

Thursday, October 28, 2010

When I finish this cup of coffee, I'm going to dump the filter and fuck the grinds. 07:04:17 AM

13 voice mails from Hendon yesterday reminding me that he was a "real" candidate. No you're not, Rickey. No you're fucking not. 07:53:13 AM

New slogan: "Your other choice is Rickey fucking Hendon. Emanuel '11." 08:08:07 AM

■ ■ ■

Axelrod just came over with a fuck-it bucket of chicken. This night just got a whole motherfucking lot better. 08:53:00 PM

The Halloween Party

Friday, October 29, 2010

Holy Jesus fucking Christ-hole, I have a massive chicken hangover. 08:36:48 AM

Shit-fucking fuck-shitters, it's motherfucking cold out here! 09:07:04 AM

■ ■ ■

Fuck you, you fucking motherfuckers, it's finally motherfucking Friday. 04:39:35 PM

Supposed to go to a Halloween party at Carl the Intern's apartment tonight. Word is Shiller's wearing a "sexy can of fruit" outfit. Fuck. 04:58:03 PM

> The "Dear First Name" intern finally got a first name of his own: Carl. As it turns out there's a cartoon called *Phineas & Ferb* that also has an intern named Carl in it. Pure coincidence—Carl is apparently just a very good name for an intern.

Also, fucking Flores is supposed to be there. Assuming he's going dressed as a ten-year-old girl because that's what he looks like anyway. 05:07:01 PM

Jody Weis is supposed to be there too. That stupid motherfucker always comes to this shit in his uniform—"I'm going as a hero." Fuck off. 05:17:09 PM

Me, I'm going as Mr. Schuester from "Glee." I love that motherfucking show so fucking much it fucking scares me sometimes. 05:40:28 PM

> There were moments in the @MayorEmanuel feed where I'd introduce an idea with the intention of picking it up again. Rahm Emanuel:

diehard *Glee* fan was one of those, but it never really came together, except for another single reference months later.

Saturday, October 30, 2010

I would try to sum up my night, but I'll just leave it at "Who wants to open up this can of fruit?" Holy shit-fucking-Christ-fuck. 08:31:14 AM

The scariest part of Halloween this year is the realization that I'm going to be voting for motherfucking Alexi in three days. BOO! 11:58:15 AM

All Hallows' Eve

Sunday, October 31, 2010

Just bought a little fake blood sprayer I can attach to my finger stump. These fucking trick-or-treat kids will shit their diapers. 09:34:34 AM

Guy came to my door in the most fucking amazing Zombie Pat Quinn outfit. Then I realized it was actually just sad-shitting Quinn himself. 02:24:59 PM

■ ■ ■

Holy fuck, I've eaten so much candy corn that I think I can see through motherfucking time! 06:09:44 PM

Caught in a fucking candy-corn haze. Jean Baptiste Point Du Sable and Papa Bear Halas are dancing. Axelrod's mustache sings like an angel. 08:51:02 PM

Du Sable was the first recorded resident of Chicago, living there in early 1790. George "Papa Bear" Halas was the head coach of the Chicago Bears from 1922 to, impossibly, 1967. His other nickname was "Mr. Everything," which is super awesome.

John Belushi and Harold Washington are swimming in the river. Their bodies bleed together in the dark murk of the water. FUCKING BEAUTIFUL. 09:04:20 PM

Harold Washington—referred to in deferential tones simply as "Harold"—was the first African-American mayor of Chicago. Elected in 1983, he died in office in 1987. Comedian John Belushi was one of the original cast members of *Saturday Night Live*. He died from a drug overdose in 1982.

I look out the window and the Hancock and the Sears reach out and kiss each other tenderly. My fucking tears taste like celery salt. 09:15:12 PM

The stars are red and the sky is striped with blue. I baptize myself in the lake's frigid waters. I AM REFUCKINGBORN. 10:32:40 PM

Monday, November 1, 2010

Where the fuck am I? What the fuck happened last night? And why the fuck am I wearing nothing but Payton's retired jersey? 08:00:45 AM

That'd be Walter "Sweetness" Payton, the legendary Chicago Bear.

I'm on a roof. All I see up here with me is the head of Benny the Bull and about 700 motherfucking Brady for Gov yard signs. Uh . . . help? 08:35:24 AM

Bill Brady was running on the Republican ticket for governor of Illinois.

OK, I'm on the roof of the Museum of Science and Industry. Axelrod's got a ladder set up. Fucking Christ, I've gotta lay off the sugar. 09:00:53 AM

The Motherfucking Midterms

I would rather wet my ballsack and stick it to a frozen fucking flagpole than vote for Quinn and Alexi tomorrow. But I will anyway. 06:41:18 PM

I know it's not a ringing fucking endorsement, but seriously: they're both as dumb as a sack of cocks. But the other guys are dumber. 06:55:21 PM

Claypool actually seems like a smart motherfucker. Or maybe it's just that Berrios makes me vomit into my fucking mouth whenever I see him. 10:36:46 PM

> Never knew the candidates in the Cook County assessor's race? Now you do: Forrest Claypool and Joe Berrios.

Tuesday, November 2, 2010

Just voted. Yep, that felt just as shitty as I thought it would. Ah, motherfucking democracy. 07:23:33 AM

■ ■ ■

Alexi just called to thank me, except it came out sounding like "Tankoo f'ya vode." I get dumber every time I talk with that motherfucker. 11:40:52 AM

■ ■ ■

Axelrod and I are debating whether it makes more sense to get drunk now or wait until West Coast polls close. Fuck it. Now. 05:59:51 PM

> The seven-o'clock polls on the East Coast were about to close. The Democratic bloodbath of the 2010 midterm elections was about to begin. And @MayorEmanuel and Axelrod were about to get very, very drunk.

I present to you the new motherfucking congressperson from Kentucky, Rand Paul. And people wondered why I got out when I did. 06:07:31 PM

> Rand Paul's Senate victory was the first of many GOP upsets of the night. The speed with which updates were happening made it difficult to keep up. That's my best excuse for my mistake of moving Paul from the Senate to the House.

Holy motherfucking Jesus fucking Christ, we do not have anywhere near enough alcohol to get us through this fucking night. 06:10:08 PM

You know, it's really not that the Republicans are going to win tonight, it's that the ones who will are all motherfucking crazy. 06:25:07 PM

Axelrod is insisting that Paul is a senator, not a congressperson. I'm insisting that he pour me another dozen drinks before I accept it. 06:34:13 PM

And my Paul mistake was corrected.

You know shit is bad when your highlight reel has to include a guy who won against a motherfucking antimasturbation ass-crazy witch. 07:21:27 PM

Delaware was announced for Democrat Chris Coons, beating GOP candidate Christine O'Donnell, who had somehow managed to spend much of the campaign explaining past antimasturbation speeches and denying that she was a witch.

The New Democratic Party: We can beat the shit out of wrestlers and witches. Regular old nutjobs? Not so fucking much. 07:36:48 PM

Connecticut was called for Democrat Richard Blumenthal, beating the Republican candidate, Linda McMahon, whose prior experience was running World Wrestling Entertainment.

Wins in Connecticut, Delaware, and West Virginia. Someone want to chalk one up in a motherfucking state that motherfucking counts? 07:55:57 PM

Fax from Plouffe is coming in now. It just reads "FUUUUUUUUUUUUUUUUUUUU . . ." I'm assuming a C-K will come in eventually. 08:03:00 PM

Axelrod just went out to get more beer and about 75 fuck-it buckets of chicken. This night calls for a good old-fashioned deep-fry wallow. 08:22:09 PM

That Rand Paul speech almost made me choke on my own motherfucking vomit. Six years of that asshole. Six fucking years. 08:25:45 PM

Contemplating snapping my cock in a mousetrap. Has to be better than the rest of these fucking results. 08:47:32 PM

Yep, it was. Might need a motherfucking Band-Aid though. 08:54:31 PM

How is it that motherfucking Colorado is emerging as the most sane fucking state in the union? 09:28:08 PM

Colorado bucked the overall anti-Democrat trend of the night, electing a Democratic governor and retaining its Democratic senator.

I know it's great if Alexi wins, but seriously: we'll all have to stare at his dumb fucking face for the next six years. 09:39:27 PM

Making a call to Feingold, trying to get that asshole over here to drink with me and Axelrod. What the fuck else does he have to do now? 09:40:34 PM

Russ Feingold, longtime reformer and political maverick, had just lost the Senate seat he had held in Wisconsin since 1993.

Seriously, Russ, it shouldn't have been motherfucking you. 09:54:52 PM

Jesus fucking Christ, I can't fucking take it. Axelrod switched over to reruns of "Night Court," and I'm not changing it back. 10:02:29 PM

Just interrupted "Night Court" to say the Dems will lose the House. Hope the next interruption is to tell me that the night is fucking dark. 10:20:11 PM

Just four years before, Emanuel had become Democratic Caucus chairman of the House after the Democrats regained control of that chamber.

If that crazy fucking motherfucking fucking Sharron fucking Angle fucking wins, I'm fucking done with motherfucking democracy. 10:27:40 PM

Sharron Angle was the GOP candidate in Nevada, looking to unseat Senate Majority Leader Harry Reid. She was, by most accounts, pretty fucking crazy.

Hey, Meg Whitman, you can buy anything, but you can't buy motherfucking backbone. 10:42:44 PM

Meg Whitman was the Republican candidate for Senate in California. It had just been announced that she had lost her self-financed $163 million campaign. Why not send her out with a nice *Rushmore* reference?

Feingold just got here. That motherfucker is seriously in a bad place. But things are looking up: "Hey, is that 'Night Court'? Awesome." 10:57:46 PM

You know, I'd feel a lot better about the Democrats retaining the goddamn Senate if they'd all pull their fucking fists out of their asses. 11:03:58 PM

I'm just going to say it right now: The Boehner/boner jokes are too fucking easy. Motherfucking amateur motherfucking hour. 11:14:53 PM

This didn't stop Twitter from lighting up with those very jokes almost immediately after John Boehner was announced as the new Speaker of the House.

Shit motherfucking fuck shitting shit fuckers. Fucking shitbagging tea shitters. Fuck fucking fuck motherfuck. Shit shitting shittingshit. 11:21:11 PM

@MayorEmanuel doesn't take lightly the announcement that the Democrats have lost Obama's former Senate seat.

Alexi was a dumb fucking sack of shit. But he was OUR dumb fucking sack of shit. 11:28:39 PM

So it comes down to hoping that Harry fucking Reid pulls off Nevada? Is there a Chicago on some tropical fucking island I can be mayor of? 11:47:26 PM

Congratulations on the win, Harry, you colossally boring, old fucking man. 11:56:54 PM

Harry Reid held his seat in Nevada, and the Democrats held onto a slim majority in the Senate.

Wednesday, November 3, 2010

Feingold passed out. I tucked his jacket around him and am letting the sad motherfucker sleep. Dream the dreams of the righteous, Russ. 12:10:04 AM

Me? I'm up all night. This "Night Court" thing turned out to be a motherfucking MARATHON. Oh Bull, you gentle fucking giant, hold us all. 12:16:28 AM

Groundhog Day

Holy fucking shit-bags. Can we get a motherfucking do-over on yesterday? 07:33:09 AM

Carl the Intern has just been sent on the mother of all coffee runs. There's going to be a world fucking shortage when he's done. 08:30:59 AM

■ ■ ■

Feingold just woke up. Not entirely clear he remembers what happened last night. I'm certainly not going to fucking tell him. 01:33:27 PM

■ ■ ■

Axelrod cleared all the newspapers, so Feingold still doesn't know. Current plan is to convince him he's fucking stuck, "Groundhog Day" style. 10:12:49 PM

Two Bill Murray film references in 24 hours.

Thursday, November 4, 2010

Filled the bathtub with coffee. About to dunk my motherfucking head in it. 07:36:42 AM

Downside to this "Groundhog Day" plan with Feingold: Axelrod's sweater really fucking smells on day three. 08:13:16 AM

■ ■ ■

Shit—who knew Russ knew how to use a computer? Now he's fucking bawling again. 10:27:21 AM

California, Dreaming

Off to the airport to head to LA for Ari's fund-raiser. I know he's my brother, but he fucking terrifies me. 10:28:09 AM

■ ■ ■

Ari met me at LAX wearing nothing but a chinchilla coat. "Are you ready for this?" he asked, grinning. No I'm fucking not. 05:01:38 PM

Ari drives his Tesla about five miles an hour. And whistles at every woman we pass. My back fucking hurts from slumping in my seat. 05:26:14 PM

■ ■ ■

"Oh, it's motherfucking on now, you fucking motherfuckers!" That's Ari, shouting from the balcony, before jumping into the pool below. 07:42:54 PM

> The fund-raiser portrayed here did indeed happen (though clearly the details are a little different). It was cohosted by Ari, David Geffen, Bob Iger (CEO of Disney), Peter Chernin (former CEO of Fox Entertainment), and Haim Saban (a media mogul whom you've probably never heard of but is credited with creating He-Man and producing the *Mighty Morphin' Power Rangers*. He's also the 102nd richest person in America).

David Geffen keeps egging him on. Geffen, by the way, travels with a pack of tiny fucking dogs. There are like 40 of them here. 07:45:05 PM

Ari has a midget walking around with a bowl strapped to his head for people to put money in. "He's your donation munchkin!!" Fuck. 07:50:55 PM

When the midget walked in, I said "Ari, no." And he said, "Look, you fucking piece of shit, at least it's not a coke mirror on his head." 07:54:31 PM

Kid Rock just showed up. I feel giddy like a motherfucking schoolgirl. 08:05:33 PM

Bob Iger just showed up wearing only a little leather pouch over his cock. Ari says that's how he's always dressed when he's not at Disney. 08:30:20 PM

You know who's fucking classy? Meryl motherfucking Streep. She didn't show, but she sent a really nice card. And $10k. 08:46:25 PM

Kid Rock and Geffen got into a fistfight. Crashed through the French doors, off the balcony, and into the pool. His dogs are jumping in too. 08:53:49 PM

Seriously there are like 70 fucking tiny dogs freaking the fuck out in the pool. Donation munchkin is trying to fish them out. There he goes. 08:57:09 PM

So now my fucking money is floating in the pool, while a midget, 80 tiny dogs, David fucking Geffen, and Kid Rock splash around. 09:00:24 PM

Jesus fucking Christ this is a fucking disaster. I should have stayed home shaking hands at your motherfucking L station. 09:11:31 PM

Iger seems to have "lost" his cock-pouch. Just fucking perfect. 09:14:58 PM

You know who's awesome? Geffen's boyfriend. Walked over, handed me a beer, and said, "Welcome to motherfucking LA. Get out while you can." 09:53:27 PM

Friday, November 5, 2010

"Wake the fuck up, you stupid fucking shitbag." Yeah, good morning to you too, Ari. I cannot wait to catch the plane home. 08:34:11 AM

Kid Rock is passed out on a lawn chair and they're still pulling Geffen's dogs out of the pool filter. But I made 500k. Good fucking haul. 08:40:28 AM

In reality, Emanuel made far more than $500k from that fund-raiser. Once his campaign finance records for Q4 were released, it was revealed that Saban alone donated $300,000.

Three things LA has that Chicago doesn't: 1) warmth; 2) a shit-ton of rich assholes willing to give me money; 3) taco trucks. 09:00:42 AM

One thing Chicago has that LA doesn't: a fucking soul. Let's head motherfucking home. 09:05:33 AM

Home Again

When I beat you, I'm not sitting down to dinner with you afterwards. I'm not having a fucking beer. When I beat you, you stay fucking beat. 04:24:55 PM

> This was the season of summits between rival candidates in Illinois. There was a "sandwich summit" between Illinois Governor Quinn and his GOP opponent Bill Brady at Manny's Deli in Chicago following the end of their contested election. This followed a "beer summit" between Giannoulias and his Republican rival Mark Kirk at Chicago's Billy Goat Tavern.

■ ■ ■

Fuck you, Chicago, it's motherfucking Friday motherfucking night. Time to go the fuck home. 05:59:33 PM

Saturday, November 6, 2010

Whoever called this motherfucking Saturday morning meeting is a motherfucking dead man. 08:26:29 AM

Sunday, November 7, 2010

Fuck you, Daylight Savings Time, fuck you right in your stupid fucking sun orbit. 08:01:52 AM

You know what's cute? That Chico thinks he has a fucking chance. Awwwww. 09:23:14 AM

> That's Gery Chico, a longtime figure in Chicago politics. He served as Daley's chief of staff for three years, and then as the board

president of the Chicago Public Schools, the Chicago Park District, and the Chicago City Colleges. Amazingly, he positioned himself as an outsider early on in this race. He ran hard against Emanuel the whole time, but in these early days tried to paint Rahm as more in line with Washington, DC, and Hollywood than Chicago. On the day Emanuel was at his brother's fund-raiser in LA, Chico held a press conference at the Hollywood Grill, a longtime diner in the Wicker Park neighborhood.

■ ■ ■

I'd be more excited about this Bears win if the experience of watching them didn't feel like stuffing a Q-tip up my fucking urethra. 03:16:21 PM

The Bears had only narrowly beaten the winless (to that point in the season) Buffalo Bills 21–19.

Beach Bums

Monday, November 8, 2010

Fucking motherfucking fuck-loving coffee. 07:29:23 AM

Today's strategy session: Do we actually pretend that Davis and Chico matter, or do we just not give a fuck? 09:21:00 AM

US Representative Danny Davis, in office since 1997, was another candidate in the mayoral race. This was not his first shot at the office, however; he had previously run against Daley in an unsuccessful bid in 1991.

■ ■ ■

Fuck you, winter! It's motherfucking incredible outside! 12:47:07 PM

It really was incredible outside, the first of a string of 60 degree–plus days in November.

Tuesday, November 9, 2010

I know I'm supposed to be shaking hands at some fucking factory, but fuck it: me and Axelrod are heading to the Oak Street Beach. You in? 09:56:41 AM

In a few weeks, you're going to be cock-deep in snow. Fuck your job and come to the motherfucking beach, you assholes. 10:08:05 AM

Axelrod in a Speedo is a motherfucking magnificent sight. 10:23:26 AM

Standing knee-deep in this fucking water, feeling the sun in my face. If someone hands me a taco al pastor, I'd be happy to fucking die here. 10:49:57 AM

If this weather holds up, I'll use my political capital in DC to change November to Nofuckingvember! With the fucking exclamation point. 11:27:07 AM

Let's Go Fly a Kite

Wednesday, November 10, 2010

Kites, people. Look at this fucking weather. Today it's motherfucking kites. 08:43:19 AM

Seriously, Axelrod and I are heading to Montrose fucking Harbor. I'll be flying the giant fucking pirate ship. Axelrod's got Hello Kitty. 08:50:50 AM

It seems like every city has a place where "kite people" congregate. Montrose Harbor, on the North Side, is Chicago's.

When Axelrod pulled up in his Civic, he was still in his fucking Speedo. "It just feels right." Fuck yes. 09:08:02 AM

■ ■ ■

I just want to bend this weather over and fuck it until it hurts.
12:31:52 PM

And you know what? You do too. NOFUCKINGVEMBER! 12:36:21 PM

Text from Plouffe: "Vacation's over, ass-wipes. Back to work
tomorrow." Axelrod just mooned my phone. 02:26:25 PM

■ ■ ■

As punishment for my taking the last two days off, Plouffe just
faxed over a press release: I'm announcing on a fucking Saturday.
Fuck me. 08:25:19 PM

> It's worth noting here that Emanuel returned to Chicago in late
> September. This "fax from Plouffe" is setting the date for his
> announcement that he'll actually be running for mayor, a month and
> a half after he arrived.

I faxed him back a picture of my cock. Fuck this motherfucking
Saturday bullshit. 08:57:52 PM

Fuckyoupon

Thursday, November 11, 2010

Motherfucking cock-bowling shit-cleaners. Where is that fuck-
crying qqcoffee? 07:41:17 AM

> Around this time, the alternate keyboard I was using on my phone—a
> beta version of Swype—really started to get terrible. That double Q
> had to be deleted countless times, but I didn't always catch them—this
> one is left in because it sets up the Tweet that follows.

Fuck, I'm so fucking tired that I can't even motherfucking typ.
07:43:55 AM

> Typo on this one entirely intentional.

■ ■ ■

You know what's wrong with motherfucking John Kass besides fucking everything? That he actually thinks that "Rahmfather" shit is clever. 07:55:08 AM

Seriously, that guy needs to shut his talentless fucking trap before he wakes up one morning to find his hairplugs stuffed up his piss hole. 07:57:43 AM

John Kass writes a column on page A2 of the *Chicago Tribune*, the spot occupied by legendary "everyman" journalist Mike Royko until he died. It is a massive understatement to say that Kass is no Royko. That said, I believe his hair is genuine.

■ ■ ■

Plouffe faxed the schedule. I'm heading to some Internet company today. Like we're going to save the fucking economy with 50% off spa days. 08:08:27 AM

■ ■ ■

Been on this Groupon tour for 20 minutes wondering why the fuck a 12-year-old is leading it. Turns out he's their CEO. 11:41:52 AM

To be fair, Andrew Mason, the CEO of the daily deals site Groupon, looks more like an 18-year-old. Impossibly, he's actually 29. Rahm visited many Chicago-based tech companies during his campaign, and Groupon, which *Forbes* once called "the fastest growing company ever," fell very much in line with his message of economic innovation.

Apparently we're saving the fucking city by thwarting child labor laws. I swear there's nobody in this building above the age of 13. 11:46:50 AM

Seriously, can someone offer these guys 50% off employees who can grow fucking pubic hair? 11:51:28 AM

Axelrod has been playing foosball while I've been dragged on this motherfucking tour. How many computers do I have to stand and look at? 12:01:20 PM

That said, I've gotten 50% off so many motherfucking manicures that my cuticles are going to motherfucking blind you. 12:11:08 PM

I actually wrote this with the intention of using the detail later. Never did get back to the blinding cuticles. Like the *Glee* reference before it, a number of things went this way—I'd leave bread crumbs, little bits that could get picked up later if the opportunity arose (or, more accurately, if I remembered I'd written them).

Hey, Chico and Davis, I got you a Fuckyoupon: 50% off getting out of this race with your dick still stitched on. 12:18:54 PM

■ ■ ■

Fax from Plouffe: Alexi's considering making a run for mayor. That's what we need: more motherfucking losers in this race. 07:41:15 PM

There was no fax. Instead, there was a report from *Chicago Sun-Times* reporter Lynne Sweet that Alexi Giannoulias was pondering entering the mayoral race. "I don't think Giannoulias is that interested in jumping in the mayor's race," Sweet wrote, "but his approach, I gather, is this: it doesn't hurt to listen to the aldermen to see what they have to say."

I swear to fucking god, Alexi enters the race and I will break my dick off and fuck him in his motherfucking exposed pores. 07:42:07 PM

I would rather debate my own fucking ballsack than have to stand at a podium across from Alexi and listen to his dumb fucking mouth. 07:47:08 PM

Hey, Alexi, I picked up a Fuckyoupon for you too: 75% off your worst motherfucking nightmare. 07:51:06 PM

Seriously, the thought of Alexi motherfucking Giannoulias entering this goddamn race makes me feel like my fucking brain is on fire. 08:02:14 PM

This City Used to Build Things

Friday, November 12, 2010

I motherfucking need some motherfucking coffee poured down my motherfucking gullet right motherfucking now. 07:43:25 AM

Strategy session for tomorrow: Axelrod says that "Why the fuck do you think I'm here, you fucking shitbags?" is "too strong" of an opener. 08:10:28 AM

Plouffe's on speaker. Says I should look "fresh faced." If that asshole ever comes to Chicago, I'm going to stick my ballsack in his eye. 08:15:36 AM

Axelrod also says no to, "I'm not here because I like you fucking twat-warts, I'm here to be your mayor." 08:30:33 AM

■ ■ ■

Touring some fucking T-shirt company today. T-shirts and coupons? This city is so fucking motherfucking fucked. 10:13:51 AM

> Rahm Emanuel visited the T-shirt company Threadless, which is based in Chicago, twice during the campaign. Threadless pioneered a vote-based system for selecting T-shirt designs that has been much imitated in the decade since it was founded.

Seriously, this city used to build things. Now we're just assholes with novelty T-shirts. I'm with motherfucking stupid. 10:34:36 AM

Axelrod's excited though: "I want the one of the cookie drinking a glass of milk." 10:42:15 AM

For the next hour I'm going to be staring blankly at T-shirts pretending like I give a fuck. 10:54:12 AM

Yeah, it really is just a giant fucking pile of T-shirts. Axelrod is wearing about half of them at this point. 11:22:31 AM

Axelrod: "Do you have any shirts with wolves on them?" That fucking guy is obsessed with wolves. 11:32:06 AM

Can't pull Axelrod away from this fucking Ping-Pong table. Maybe I need to leave a trail of T-shirts leading out the door, bread-crumb style. 12:05:52 PM

■ ■ ■

I see Alexi got that Fuckyoupon I sent over. Mason was right: the real profit is when they don't redeem them. 01:58:09 PM

> As quickly as the rumor started that Alexi was entering the race, another began that he was out.

■ ■ ■

Finally got Axelrod away from the Ping-Pong. Never need to look at another motherfucking T-shirt again. 04:06:28 PM

Action Items: (1) fucking (2) finally (3) it's fucking (4) motherfucking (5) Friday (6) fucking (7) night. 04:32:42 PM

The Fucking Announcement

Saturday, November 13, 2010

Jesus motherfucking Christ, this goddamn Saturday morning announcement is going to motherfucking kill me. COFFEE. 09:21:33 AM

> It was the morning of Emanuel's official announcement that he'd be running for mayor of Chicago. He held it at the John C. Coonley School in the city's North Center neighborhood.

The only thing that's going to get me through this is knowing that when I shake your hand, mine is covered in cock sweat. 09:44:32 AM

> This is almost a word-for-word match to a Tweet back when @MayorEmanuel was leaving Washington, DC. I'd remembered that line and wanted to use something similar because, at that point, the @MayorEmanuel was being followed by probably ten times more people than the first time around. That said, I never realized just how close a match it was until now.

We were supposed to do this at 10, but it's going to take a motherfucking hour to navigate through all these fucking baby strollers. Go home. 09:58:51 AM

■ ■ ■

Thank fucking god: Axelrod slipped me a couple fucking shots just now. Here goes motherfucking nothing. 11:06:02 AM

Speech preview: I've spent these last weeks listening to your problems. And gone home every fucking night and poured bleach in my ears. 11:12:03 AM

Speech preview: Despite all of you, I still want to be the motherfucking mayor. 11:23:57 AM

Christ-sucking cock-holes, that was 45 minutes I will never, fucking ever, get back. 11:46:12 AM

And now I have to stand around kissing all of your fucking asses while the weather turns from shitty to motherfucking miserable. Fuck this. 11:47:35 AM

■ ■ ■

Axelrod and I are heading over for a celebratory meal at Superdawg. I am going to eat the living shit out of a motherfucking Whoopskidawg. 06:58:58 PM

> The Superdawg drive-in, located on the northwest side of the city, features statues of two giant anthropomorphized hot dogs on its roof. Their names—because *of course they're named*—are Maurie and Flaurie, after the original owner and his wife.

Sunday, November 14, 2010

Sleeping motherfucking in today. No more listening tour for you assholes means more sleep for me. Fuck yes. 10:49:50 AM

> While Emanuel's official announcement as a mayoral candidate meant that he was no longer officially on a listening tour, it didn't stop him from continuing to visit L stops, bars, and eateries every day of the campaign.

Filing Day at the Grease Monkey

Monday, November 15, 2010

Picked up a Fuckyoupon for Meeks this weekend: 50% off nobody gives a fuck. 08:30:34 AM

Axelrod's Civic broke an axle on the way to file our petitions today, so Carl the Intern had to steal a cart from Jewel and walk 'em in. 08:38:56 AM

> November 15 was the first day to file petitions to get on the ballot with the Chicago Board of Election Commissioners. Order on the ballot is set on a first-come, first-served basis, so the strategy is to get in line early. One caveat is that all candidates in the lineup by the time the office opens get dibs on the top spot, which is then decided by a lottery.

Meanwhile, we're over at the Grease Monkey trying not to get completely fucked on the axle replacement. 08:40:15 AM

What the fucking fuck is a "constant velocity joint" and can we get by without one? 08:52:04 AM

Before he wheeled off with our petitions, I gave Carl head-fake lessons. Chico is about to get the head-faking of a fucking lifetime. 09:03:13 AM

Axelrod's Civic already gets by without passenger-side windows or radio. Does it really need a differential seal? 09:07:13 AM

Carl just called Axelrod's Razr: cart tipped over on Washington; most of the petitions ended up in the street. Not my fucking day. 09:15:44 AM

Carl says he got most of the petitions and that they're "mostly just muddy." At least that'll cover the coffee I spilled on them. 09:22:12 AM

Shit is so fucking motherfucking fucked that I keep fucking forgetting to fucking swear. Fuck. 09:26:32 AM

■ ■ ■

Finally getting Axelrod's car out of the shop. Motherfuck. Carl says Moseley Braun was crowing about having the most signatures. Fuck her. 05:57:12 PM

All Moseley Braun's signatures and two bucks will buy her is a Coke. No idea how much it'd cost her to buy a fucking clue. 05:59:07 PM

Beep Beep, Motherfucker

Tuesday, November 16, 2010

Holy fucking Jesus fuck. Where the fucking fuck is the motherfucking coffee? 07:35:22 AM

When I was a dancer, I learned the phrase "mutually assured destruction." Meeks, Davis, and Braun should fucking look it up. 10:06:21 AM

> Much of the media narrative at this point was around which of the three candidates would become the "consensus candidate" for Chicago's large African-American population. This was also an ongoing story between Chico and Del Valle and about which one would represent Chicago's Hispanic community.

■ ■ ■

Been driving with the Teamsters all day. Pulled up to Chico's house in a big rig and blew on the horn. Beep beep, motherfucker! 05:08:49 PM

> In the real race, November 16 marked the release of a Teamsters-sponsored poll that showed Emanuel capturing 34%. The next closest candidate, Davis, was at 14%, marking a 20% gap between the two— that would be one of the closest gaps of the entire campaign.

Another thing about the Teamsters: you have not eaten a sandwich until you have eaten a motherfucking Teamster sandwich. 05:23:25 PM

Hanging with Teamsters is like hanging with high school kids, but with mustaches. You just eat, drink, and fucking drive around. 06:06:34 PM

Axelrod and this Teamster named Bruno are in the mother of all pizza-eating contests. Fucking I kid you not: we're in hour three. 09:45:29 PM

Wednesday, November 17, 2010

Axelrod's been puking most of the night. The price of motherfucking victory. 08:15:53 AM

Hanging out with beat cops today, as my motherfucking Chicago mustache tour continues. Tomorrow: cartoon Italian plumbers. 09:07:58 AM

One of the worst stories written about the @MayorEmanuel account once my identity had been revealed misrepresented the mustache tour as "meeting with Italians and Teamsters." Clearly, the journalist had never played Super Mario Brothers.

■ ■ ■

He keeps this residency shit up, and I'm going to cram my motherfucking mortgage documents right up Ed Burke's pockmarked ass. 11:39:57 AM

One of the major questions at this stage in the race—one that would plague Emanuel for months—was whether or not he was actually a resident of Chicago. Because he moved to Washington, DC, to serve the president—after serving in the House of Representatives as a congressperson from Chicago's Ravenswood neighborhood—the legal argument was that he was no longer a resident of Illinois, and thus could not run for office. Power brokers and competing candidates began to press the residency issue, mostly behind the scenes. Though no one candidate or figure ever stepped forward to orchestrate the lawsuits that would follow, the *Chicago Sun-Times* portrayed Ed Burke's support for pursuing Emanuel's residency issues as "a poorly kept secret."

■ ■ ■

I'm not saying Daley's a bad guy, but his new budget just fucked you in the ass without even saying please. 05:23:41 PM

> Mayor Daley released his final budget, which closed a gaping deficit by raiding the $1.15 billion fund from the 75-year parking meter lease. Only three years after signing the deal, there was only $76 million remaining in the account.

Next parking meter box you see, whip your cock out and fuck the coin return. Coin-slot sex is the only thing you'll see from the meter deal. 05:33:12 PM

I mean really, how the fuck do you fucking twat-up a seventy-five-year lease deal? Just a few coins motherfucking left over? Fuck this shit. 05:57:24 PM

So now we're all running to be mayor of a city that's so fucking motherfucking broke, we'll all be selling plasma to fund the schools. Fuck. 06:05:38 PM

Movie Night (part one)

Thursday, November 18, 2010

Staffing up with a new intern, who just walked in with motherfucking tea. Hey what's-your-fuck, you're out. 07:36:28 AM

Axelrod's already getting his motherfucking Hagrid costume together for the "Deathly Hallows" opening at midnight. 08:01:39 AM

I keep telling Axelrod that I'm going as Gandalf. He's getting so fucking mad I think his mustache might fall off. 08:09:06 AM

> Gandalf is, of course, a wizard from the *Lord of the Rings* series, not the *Harry Potter* series.

Strategy session, and every motherfucking suggestion from Axelrod involves a fucking Harry Potter reference. 08:24:33 AM

Fuck: "Let's cast lumos on the budget situation." 08:25:44 AM

In case you've somehow avoided Harry Potter (and good on you if you have), lumos is a spell that causes the tip of your magic wand to light up.

Motherfuck: "Let's use stupefy on Chico." 08:27:17 AM

And stupefy is a stunning spell, used to incapacitate enemies.

I know it's only 8:30, but I need a motherfucking drink. 08:31:06 AM

■ ■ ■

Axelrod spent most of the 2:30 meeting "getting all of you up to speed on the Harry Potter franchise." Can it fucking be midnight yet? 03:17:51 PM

3/4 of the way through his retelling, he started crying because Dumbledore was killed. And he hasn't fucking stopped bawling since. 03:19:47 PM

I swear, by the end of this day, I may just stuff this motherfucking wand in my motherfucking ear hole. 03:24:45 PM

■ ■ ■

This line is fucking long and fucking cold. And this fucking wizard's cloak is not magically fucking warm. 08:30:22 PM

Friday, November 19, 2010

Jesus motherfucking Christ, I have a hangover the size of fucking Hogwarts. 08:38:11 AM

Back to the Grind

Meeks, you keep pushing this residency bullshit and I will cram your cross so far up your ass, it'll take three days just to fucking find it. 08:43:41 AM

I will admit that I'm a resident of Theothermotherfuckersaremother fuckingdisasters-ville. 08:53:47 AM

And I own a timeshare in the great city of Fuckyouton. 08:55:11 AM

The first fucking person to file a suit over my residency is going to find my foot taking up residency inside their sphincter. 09:00:09 AM

■ ■ ■

Fuck you all of you motherfuckers in the motherfucking asshole, it's finally motherfucking Friday night. 04:53:17 PM

Axelrod is off at his sixth screening of "Deathly Hallows," but Penny Pritzker's bringing over a diamond-encrusted bucket of chicken. Fuck yes. 05:11:40 PM

Penny also brought over four cans of Four Loko and is offering me $100k for each one I drink. Easy fucking money. 05:39:46 PM

> Four Loko was a briefly famous alcoholic beverage that combined malt liquor with a fruit-flavored caffeinated energy drink. The FDA issued a warning to the manufacturers of Four Loko, on November 17, that the addition of caffeine to alcoholic beverages was an "unsafe food additive," which kicked off a ban in many states and cities.

■ ■ ■

Sho thag for logos shtit aignt sho fuctink touf. 08:17:28 PM

> "So that Four Lokos shit ain't so fucking tough."

Im sho fuctink fukt on thiz resgidetse shid itz nod efin fungky. 08:27:30 PM

> "I'm so fucking fucked on this residency shit it's not even funny."

Saturday, November 20, 2010

Motherfucking fucking fuck fuckers. 08:04:26 AM

■ ■ ■

The decision to only use one end zone in this fucking NU game was made by fucking cocktards. Dumbest fucking game ever. 04:45:44 PM

> Northwestern (Emanuel's alma mater) played the University of Illinois in a game held at Wrigley Field, the home of the Chicago Cubs and, for 50 years, the home of the Chicago Bears as well. Because of the configuration of the football field on the baseball diamond, and the distance to the wall from the end zone (in parts, just six inches), Big Ten officials ruled that all offensive play would go in one direction. Which, you know, is kind of weird.

Sunday, November 21, 2010

Going over Thanksgiving plans with Axelrod today. He's saying Harold's, I'm saying Popeye's. Fucking fuck. 08:52:36 AM

> Harold's Chicken Shack is a Chicago fried-chicken chain. It was founded in 1950 by Harold Pierce, and there are more than 62 Harold's Chicken Shacks in existence now. Harold's chicken shacks are numbered, but the system is slightly random (for instance, the first shack was #11). Because of the way the franchise agreements are written, there are actually wild inconsistencies between the Shacks, and connoisseurs debate which is the best. The most scientific ranking of all Harold's Shacks, which was undertaken by journalist Mike Sula in 2006, found that Harold's No. 55, at 100 West 87th Street, was mathematically the best Shack in the city.

Jesus motherfucking Christ, could it be any more gray and fucking miserable outside? Fuck this shit: stay in. 08:01:18 AM

Monday, November 22, 2010

Carl has hooked up the motherfucking coffee IV, so I might be able to overcome this fucking gray fucking day. 08:38:31 AM

■ ■ ■

I hope this motherfucking monsoon floods the shit out of my former house. Learn to swim, you piece of shit. 06:17:22 PM

> Almost two inches of rain fell on November 22.

I pissed myself laughing at the idea of a motherfucking "Draft Burris Movement." I may vote for that fuck, so he at least gets one.
06:20:40 PM

Roland Burris, who was selected by Rod Blagojevich to temporarily fill Barack Obama's Senate seat—following all the controversy involved in Blago's alleged attempts to sell the seat—had mayoral petitions filed on his behalf by a "Draft Burris Movement." He never really got past the filing stage and eventually would quietly withdraw.

Personally, I see this as a three-way race now: Me, M. Tricia Lee, and all the other sorry fucking assholes. 06:27:31 PM

There were a number of characters who filed petitions to get on the ballot; one of the most interesting was Lee, a "fourth generation Chicagoan" who offered a unique platform that centered around building two city halls, one for the South and East Sides and one for the North and West Sides. It turns out that she actually lived in Oak Lawn but had used the address of a motel within the city limits on her candidacy papers.

I just keep looking at this motherfucking list of candidates and thinking how it all ended up fucking circus clowns. 10:53:03 PM

Tuesday, November 23, 2010

Holy Jesus fuck, Carl the Intern forgot to pay the heating bill, so we're all fucking huddled around a goddamn hot pot right now.
09:15:59 AM

Trying to squeeze out shits that look like turkey legs, to bring to Chico's potluck. 09:58:35 AM

Hey, Chico, I would rather be endorsed by Ed Burke's cum rag than anyone connected with the motherfucking Chicago Public Schools.
04:31:28 PM

Chico received the endorsement of ex-CPS CEO Paul Vallas, who at one time had considered running for governor of Illinois, mayor of Chicago, and even president of the Cook County Board. He was the head of the public schools from 1995 to 2001 and has been cited with improving the system that had been called the "worst in the nation" by US Secretary of Education William Bennett in 1987.

During the NOLA mayor's race, candidates didn't try to get Hurricane Katrina's motherfucking endorsement. But fucking CPS is OK? 04:56:16 PM

■ ■ ■

Axelrod just walked in looking like the motherfucking Deerhunter. Looked me dead in the eye and said, "We bag a bird tomorrow." 09:58:02 PM

Turkey Hunt

Wednesday, November 24, 2010

On the way to Wisconsin with Axelrod and Carl the Intern to kill a turkey. Carl's crying. Fucking vegetarians. 08:11:15 AM

Jesus fucking Christ: Kenosha, Wisconsin, is a place I never need to go again in my motherfucking life. 09:12:09 AM

> Kenosha, Wisconsin, is the first major town north of the Illinois border along Lake Michigan.

Axelrod's been driving this whole time with a knife clenched between his teeth, like he's some kind of motherfucking pirate. 09:22:22 AM

Details, details: The knife, it turns out, is the only tool Axelrod brought for the hunt. He's chasing birds around a field, knife raised. 10:45:17 AM

Holy fuck, he got one! Now he's standing there yelling "BATHE IN THE BLOOD OF THE BIRD!" 11:51:19 AM

There is so much more blood in a turkey than you'd think. Jesus fucking Christ. 03:06:47 PM

Axelrod, me, Carl, and the Civic are completely covered in blood. If we get pulled over, this could get motherfucking ugly. 03:25:04 PM

■ ■ ■

Plouffe just faxed over the menu for tomorrow. Turns out we picked up the wrong fucking stuffing. **Motherfuck.** 06:08:24 PM

There are 100,000 fucking assholes crammed into this Dominick's. Get me my stuffing or I'll give you something to be fucking thankful **for.** 06:12:40 PM

They are out of motherfucking stuffing. Fuck every single one of you fucking goddamn motherfuckers right in your fucking face. 06:35:58 PM

■ ■ ■

Fucking Ari: "Hey, you asshole, I heard you bagged a bird. I'm sending my jet your way. Turkey day in LA—Pants fucking optional." 08:49:11 PM

Thanksgiving in LA

Thursday, November 25, 2010

"Happy fucking Thanksgiving, you motherfucking ass-hats." That's Ari, greeting us as the limo pulled up to his house. 08:53:17 AM

■ ■ ■

I've spent most of the day chasing Geffen's dogs around the goddamn house. They keep jumping up and grabbing shit off the **counters.** 08:43:49 PM

For dinner tonight, we've got Ari, Geffen & boyfriend, me, Axelrod, Carl the Intern, Carol Burnett, Harrison fucking Ford, and Kanye **West.** 08:53:13 PM

Chicago hip-hop artist Kanye West became a bit character in the narrative at this point, making multiple appearances. His album, *My Beautiful Dark Twisted Fantasy*, had just been released on November 22 and was at the front of my mind.

Carol's been drinking for like five hours now, and Harrison's been sulking in a corner for some fucking reason. 08:55:19 PM

Dinner was supposed to start an hour ago. I swear to god, I'm going to just start gnawing off my own fucking arm. 08:56:43 PM

We're late because Carl the Intern was playing football with Geffen's boyfriend and knocked over the fucking turkey deep fryer. 09:01:25 PM

Carol keeps hitting on David Geffen and nobody has the heart to tell her she'd have a better shot at a bowl of cranberry sauce. 09:04:58 PM

Kanye keeps bragging that his green bean casserole will "knock you on your ass." 09:11:35 PM

This whole fucking dinner is a goddamn waiting game on Axelrod and his motherfucking deep fried turkey. Any fucking time now. 09:15:53 PM

Fuck this. Me and Carol and Kanye are off to find a motherfucking taco truck. 09:32:36 PM

Carol Burnett's ordering tacos for the three of us—combo of cabeza, tripa, and buche. She fucking calls it "The Hot Mess." 10:11:20 PM

Sitting on a curb with Kanye West, Carol Burnett, a pile of tacos and a bottle of Hennessy. Happy motherfucking Thanksgiving. 10:19:02 PM

Friday, November 26, 2010

Stayed out all night with Carol and Kanye, just walking the fuck around. Now we're hitting the stores. BLACK FUCKING FRIDAY!!! 08:29:09 AM

Holy fuck, Carol got the greatest deal on a back massager I have ever fucking seen in my life. 09:03:57 AM

And Kanye got like fucking 80% off an amazing fucking set of bathroom towels. Bed Bath & Beyond FTMFW. 09:04:37 AM

■ ■ ■

Got back to Ari's with my rental Yaris stuffed with half-price DVDs, and Axelrod's standing there: "Your residency is challenged." Fuck me. 04:41:11 PM

> The challenges to Emanuel's residency began to roll in the day after Thanksgiving. By the end of it, more than 30 people had challenged his residency, based on the fact that section 3.1-10-5 of the Illinois Municipal Code states, "A person is not eligible for an elective municipal office unless that person is a qualified elector of the municipality and has resided in the municipality at least one year next preceding the election or appointment." While that seems cut-and-dried—Emanuel did not live in Chicago the year prior to announcing his candidacy—another section of the code states, "No elector or spouse shall be deemed to have lost his or her residence in any precinct or election district in this State by reason of his or her absence on business of the United States, or of this State." The argument made by election law attorney Burt Odelson, the most vocal of the challengers, was that the intention of that clause was and is for military service.

I'm going to watch two DVDs, eat a motherfucking In-N-Out, check out Kanye's dolphin tank, then get on a plane and fight this shit. FUCK. 04:52:45 PM

■ ■ ■

Jesus fucking Christ, dolphins are motherfucking graceful fucking animals. 07:22:30 PM

Saturday, November 27, 2010

Strategy session: Just how fucked are the fucking fucks that are trying to fuck us? Very fucking fucked. 03:26:06 PM

Sunday, November 28, 2010

Heading down to heckle Meeks at his church. He wants to fuck with where I live, I'll fuck him right back. 09:42:02 AM

> So here's the thing about the residency challenges: nobody ever took credit for coordinating them or otherwise orchestrating them. All

accusations by @MayorEmanuel, such as this reference to Meeks, were pure fiction, best I know.

Alright, front row, asshole. Motherfucking god me, you stupid motherfucker. 10:45:07 AM

Birthday Pony

Half hour until it's my motherfucking birthday. You fucking motherfuckers had better have gotten me something fucking nice. 11:32:44 PM

Monday, November 29, 2010

MOTHERFUCKING MIDNIGHT. IT'S MY MOTHERFUCKING BIRTHDAY MOTHERFUCKERS. 12:00:07 AM

■ ■ ■

Carl the Intern gave me the biggest cup of coffee I've ever seen. It's motherfucking enormous! I'm crying like a baby here. 07:58:14 AM

Fuck yes: Axelrod brought over a stuffed bear holding a "happy birthday" balloon. I named him Peaches. 08:38:45 AM

Fax from Plouffe: "I got you just what you wanted: an election lawyer that would make Jesus piss his fucking robes." 08:43:57 AM

Axelrod keeps telling me there's a "secret birthday surprise" later. It's always motherfucking Chuck E. Cheese. 09:08:05 AM

Also, Axelrod got spinner rims for his Civic and is trying to pass them off as a present for me. "But you'll look awesome." 09:16:50 AM

Meeks, Chico, and Burris have each sent fake residency papers with the note, "I got you what you really wanted." Real fucking funny. 12:48:41 PM

Braun just sent flowers though, because she's motherfucking classy. 12:49:31 PM

I'd expect that Davis will get the memo that it's my birthday in about six weeks, and issue a statement in three more. Slow motherfucker. 12:52:36 PM

■ ■ ■

Holy fuck: Axelrod's surprise gift is a bar of Ex-Lax and the key to the motherfucking city council chamber. 05:10:09 PM

Between the Ex-Lax and these two boxes of Fiber One, I'm going to be able to craft the fucking Burnham Plan of shit. 05:18:36 PM

> The Burnham Plan is a city planning document crafted by legendary urban planner and architect Daniel Burnham. Crafted over 100 years ago, it is still spoken of in hushed tones.

Birthday: (1) take a shit in the council chambers; (2) pick up Penny Pritzker and Samurai Mike Singletary; (3) taco pizza at Chuck E. Cheese. 05:39:17 PM

> "Samurai" Mike Singletary was one of the leading defensive linemen in the 1985 Super Bowl Champion Chicago Bears.

Heading over to the city council chambers now. I've got to admit: Axelrod's rims do look motherfucking sweet. 05:54:45 PM

My ass is a brown fountain of motherfucking justice! Best birthday ever!! 06:10:17 PM

■ ■ ■

Took a while longer to finish up in the city council than I thought. But I'll tell you this: that shit was a motherfucking masterpiece. 08:05:18 PM

As a result, we were late picking up Penny and Samurai Mike. They'd been drinking the whole time they were waiting. Fucking amazing. 08:06:04 PM

You haven't fucking lived until you've heard Penny Pritzker do her rendition of the "Samurai Mike" rap from the Super Bowl Shuffle. 08:14:40 PM

Mike Singletary is up on stage with that motherfucking Chuck E. Cheese robot mouse. I think Axelrod may choke, he's laughing so hard. 08:29:32 PM

This trip to Chuck E. Cheese just confirms it: I am the motherfucking king of whack-a-mole! 09:27:55 PM

Driving Lake Shore Drive in Axelrod's Civic, rain coming in the missing window. Penny, Samurai Mike, and I just fucking freestyling. YES. 10:49:02 PM

"The clock's tickin', I just count the hours / Stop trippin', I'm trippin' off the power / Till then, fuck that—the world's OURS." 10:56:55 PM

Stumbling into bed. Wet, hoarse, happy. Fifty-one is going to be all fucking right. 11:36:26 PM

Tuesday, November 30, 2010

Post-birthday hangover means that I'm going to make Meeks see motherfucking god for this shit he's pulling with my tenant. 08:19:01 AM

> One sideshow of the campaign that didn't appear in many of the @MayorEmanuel storylines (because, honestly, it disgusted me personally) was that Rob Halpin, the tenant living in Rahm Emanuel's house, was actually himself briefly a candidate for mayor. In a city that's well known for political dirty tricks, this felt like an especially dirty one. There is, however, no known connection between Meeks and Halpin.

If you are running for mayor of Chicago, do not fuck with me today. I will take this ice pack off my head and chop your fucking dick off. 08:26:10 AM

■ ■ ■

Strategy session: we're going to contest everything up to and including the existence of the motherfucking City of Chicago. 10:25:43 AM

So 21 Chicagoans have filed objections to my candidacy. The other 2,853,093 think I'm fucking amazing. I can live with that. 04:25:10 PM

Hanukkah

Wednesday, December 1, 2010

Fuck this motherfucking snow right in its motherfucking nimbostratus cloud formation. 08:41:25 AM

Axelrod's been standing outside, shovel in hand, for three hours now, like he's Nanook of the fucking North. 08:52:23 AM

There was not actually much snow that day.

I have so much fucking Hanukkah shopping to finish. Fuck this motherfucking lunar calendar bullshit. 09:29:43 AM

■ ■ ■

All this "starting at sundown" shit would be a lot fucking easier if sundown wasn't in the middle of the goddamn afternoon. 04:14:28 PM

Jesus fucking Christ, it turns out that Carl the Intern used to hustle kids on the dreidel back in Hebrew school. 06:47:44 PM

Thanks to him, we're up to our ears in fucking Hanukkah gelt. 06:53:26 PM

Thursday, December 2, 2010

Holy fucking motherfucking fuck, where the fucking fuck is the motherfucking coffee. 07:48:31 AM

Danny Davis would be a worthy motherfucking opponent if it was 1982. 07:58:32 AM

And Gery Chico would be a threat if we were running for president of the fucking PTA. 07:59:55 AM

And Braun would have a lock if we were competing for placement on a motherfucking Trivial Pursuit card. 08:01:51 AM

New slogan: "It's 2010, this is for mayor, and Trivial Pursuit is for fucking pussies. Vote Emanuel." 08:09:49 AM

■ ■ ■

Keep me locked in this room with David Hoffman much longer and I'm
going to turn into a fucking arsenic-eating life-form too. 01:41:43 PM

> Twofer alert—NASA announced the discovery of an arsenic-eating
> bacteria in a salt lake in California at the same time that Emanuel
> held a press conference with David Hoffman to unveil his ethics
> plan. Hoffman lost the Democratic Senate primary against Alexi
> Giannoulias. Prior to that losing bid, Hoffman had been a federal
> prosecutor and, later, inspector general for the City of Chicago—
> where he investigated hiring practices within city hall. He is, if truth
> be told, exactly the guy you'd want to help you write an ethics plan.

Seriously, there is a reason this guy lost to dumb-fucking Alexi. And
that reason is he is a motherfucking painfully boring motherfucker.
01:58:35 PM

Seriously, I just look at that motherfucker and I get sleepy. They
should stand him outside mattress stores. Make a fucking fortune.
02:03:29 PM

Sure, he's a fucking stand-up guy, and I'm fucking glad he's on ou
. . . zzzzzzzzzzzzz. 02:12:50 PM

■ ■ ■

Jesus fucking Christ, I almost burnt the motherfucking house down
lighting that second candle. 06:35:49 PM

Friday, December 3, 2010

Motherfuck! The! Sleep! Of! Hoffman! Is! The! Greatest! Sleep! Of!
All! Motherfucking! Time! Hoff! Me! Again! Motherfucker! 07:59:32 AM

You know what's just fucking adorable? That Ed Burke still thinks
he fucking matters. 09:38:02 AM

Axelrod just ripped the bumper off his Civic trying to attach a
fucking plow to it. "Just trying to be prepared." 10:31:30 AM

> Weather reports were promising four to eight inches of snow in the
> Chicago area, the first big snow of the year.

■ ■ ■

What are you waiting for? Motherfuck every fucking thing, it's Friday fucking night! No snow yet, you assholes; get out there! 05:11:43 PM

RIMFP

Saturday, December 4, 2010

Fuck this snow. Fuck this snow. Fuck this motherfucking snow. 08:04:30 AM

> I was actually in Phoenix, Arizona, this weekend, and had to rely on a weather app on my phone and news from my wife to know what the snow situation was.

I'm out here fucking shoveling this shit myself because Axelrod has been fucking catatonic since he heard motherfucking Ron Santo died. 08:09:35 AM

> Ron Santo played third base for the Chicago Cubs from 1960 to 1974, and later was the radio announcer for the team, where he billed himself as "the single Biggest Cubs fan of all time." He died December 3 of complications from bladder cancer and diabetes.

Worst fucking part is that I'm out here in fucking wingtips because my motherfucking boots are in the attic of my fucking rented house. 08:25:00 AM

My feet are so fucking numb that I'm considering setting them on fucking fire. 10:02:40 AM

Also, Carl the Intern won't make me a hot cocoa because he's sitting shivah with Axelrod over Santo. Fuck me. 10:03:46 AM

■ ■ ■

Axelrod's outside now with a chainsaw carving a motherfucking Ron Santo ice sculpture right now. 02:54:35 PM

Sunday, December 5, 2010

Dug out Axelrod's Civic to go buy some boots. Put fucking five lawn chairs and an old ironing board in the spot. 10:50:38 AM

> In Chicago, if you shovel the snow out of your parking space, you fill it with some crap from your basement (typically lawn chairs), which marks it as yours. It's informally called the "dibs" system, and every year there are news reports of stabbings and deaths over moving someone's dibs pile and parking in their space. If you're not from Chicago, that was probably the craziest sentence you've ever read. If you're from here, you're just nodding and saying, "I'd do it too."

We drove by Chico's house and I pissed "Fuck you you fucking motherfucker" in the snow. 01:24:22 PM

Monday, December 6, 2010

Motherfucking coffee fucking commence! 07:52:42 AM

Standing in front of City Hall, giving the fucking double birds to all these dumb fucks walking into the Board of Election office. 10:11:32 AM

> The Chicago Board of Election began to sort through the ballot challenges, though Emanuel's first hearing wouldn't be for another week.

■ ■ ■

Elizabeth Edwards was fucking classy—too bad her husband was such a fucking douche-cock. And also about the cancer. 05:15:28 PM

> News had just broken that Elizabeth Edwards, ex-wife of former presidential candidate John Edwards, was no longer treating her cancer.

Tuesday, December 7, 2010

Holy fuck, it's motherfucking cold as motherfucking shit outside. 08:04:05 AM

So my tenant isn't running for mayor after all. What a fucking motherfucking shock. 10:24:36 AM

Just hours before the Chicago Board of Elections reviewed his petition, Rob Halpin withdrew his name.

It warms my asshole to see dumb motherfuckers get kicked off the ballot. 10:40:08 AM

■ ■ ■

I would rather hang out with Elizabeth Edwards' corpse than have to go to one of these motherfucking "mayoral forums." 06:10:00 PM

It was announced that Elizabeth Edwards had died.

Too motherfucking soon? 06:15:28 PM

But really, these fucking candidate forums look absolutely motherfucking awful. 06:20:12 PM

There were dozens of mayoral forums—less formal than debates, usually focused around a single topic, and organized by a group interested in that topic. Especially in this early stage of the campaign, they attracted many of the down-ballot candidates. Emanuel did not attend a single one.

Wednesday, December 8, 2010

I would rather stick my dick to a frozen fucking flagpole than answer another motherfucking residency question. 09:07:34 AM

Axelrod has replaced all his Santo candles with Elizabeth candles. Rough fucking week for that guy. 09:18:48 AM

■ ■ ■

Axelrod's taking his heartbreak out in ice sculpture: joining Santo is Elizabeth Edwards, a unicorn, and a fucking sweet T-Rex. 02:50:19 PM

Also, he's got a fucking knitted mustache pouch to keep his 'stache warm. 02:51:56 PM

■ ■ ■

Spending the last night of Hanukkah with David Hoffman. It might be Yom fucking Kippur by the time he gets all eight candles lit. 05:24:14 PM

Jesus fucking Christ, I'm really hoping this liquor I've got can last for eight fucking days, because I may be trapped here that long. 05:49:29 PM

At this point, I'm holding my hand above the menorah, just to feel something. 06:22:37 PM

Hoffman finally got the final candle lit. That guy sure does know a lot about the motherfucking Maccabees. Fuck me. 08:18:53 PM

The Residency Hearings

Thursday, December 9, 2010

Strategy session for residency hearing: Axelrod says no to pulling my cock out and asking, "You want this shit Chicago style?". 07:49:48 AM

He also says no to pulling down my pants, spreading my cheeks and saying "Eat my motherfucking deep dish." 07:56:30 AM

■ ■ ■

Getting ready for the residency hearing tomorrow by drinking every motherfucking thing in the kitchen. Up next: Baileys and dish soap. 06:45:14 PM

Motherfucking pro tip: soy sauce and fucking cognac. Motherfucking amazing. 07:53:16 PM

Axelrod is doing yogurt and beer shooters. 08:09:25 PM

Friday, December 10, 2010

Holy fucking fuck, I need some motherfucking coffee poured directly into my fucking mouth right this motherfucking second. 08:05:44 AM

■ ■ ■

Fucking annoying hearing today that leads to even more motherfucking annoying hearings next week. Democracy is a bitch. 04:21:44 PM

Fax from Plouffe : "We need to work on your likeability before your testimony." Faxed him back a picture of my asshole. 04:39:48 PM

I don't give a thousand fucking fucks; it is motherfucking finally Friday night. 05:15:14 PM

Saturday, December 11, 2010

Axelrod and I are filling the house with donuts and seeing if we can eat our motherfucking way out. 09:56:02 AM

■ ■ ■

Motherfuck this motherfucking rain. 02:22:03 PM

Sunday, December 12, 2010

Axelrod was waking us up every hour last night as part of his "readiness patrol" and not a single fucking flake hit the goddamn ground. 08:22:25 AM

I'm so tired I think I'm going to vomit, and now it's motherfucking snowing like a motherfuck. 08:46:51 AM

Carl the Intern scheduled a fucking presser about education in the middle of a goddamn snowstorm and the motherfucking Bears game. 11:48:41 AM

Pretty sure it's payback for making Carl follow Chico around this week pretending to record him, just to fucking fuck with Chico's head. 11:50:49 AM

Gery Chico had released a video earlier in the week that showed campaign workers for Emanuel surreptitiously videotaping Chico campaign appearances. He titled the video "Transparency: Rahm Style."

■ ■ ■

Fuck this motherfucking football game. Fuck it right in its snowy motherfucking ass. 04:03:33 PM

> This was the first live-tweeted game I did. Earlier in the week, Bears safety Danieal Manning visited my son's grade school, and he came home and announced that he was now a football fan. He hung the free poster they gave him up on his wall and memorized the game dates. He begged to watch the game, so we did.

Motherfucking fucking fuck fuckers. What the fucking fuck game is fucking Cutler fucking playing? 04:24:08 PM

I'm going to go outside and have Axelrod whip iceballs at my cock. Has to be more fun than this motherfucking football game. 04:38:51 PM

Motherfucking Cutler is a motherfucking cocktard. 05:55:35 PM

> The Bears were blown out by the New England Patriots, 36–7.

Monday, December 13, 2010

Who the fuck replaced Chicago with the motherfucking ice planet Hoth? 07:58:45 AM

> Single-digit temperatures ruled the day. It was cold enough to want to crawl inside a Tauntaun to keep warm.

I know it might not send the right message, but we're taking the Imperial Walker to get to the residency hearing. Fuck the Tauntauns. 08:29:48 AM

Axelrod just got in from gassing up the Walker and his mustache looks like it was part of the Shackleton expedition. Icicles. 08:54:02 AM

> Ernest Shackleton was one of the great Antarctic explorers of the early 20th century.

■ ■ ■

Carl the Intern is cramming for tomorrow's testimony with me while Axelrod is out on a pizza run. Going to be a late motherfucking night. 06:05:10 PM

Emanuel was giving his testimony in the residency hearings the next day. And @MayorEmanuel was spending the night boning up on Chicago facts, as if he were taking a US citizenship exam.

Did you know there are 77 communities in Chicago? Motherfucking take THAT, Board of Election Commissioners! 06:13:04 PM

Chicago derives its name from the motherfucking Miami-Illinois tribal word for "wild onion." Fuck yes: *shikaakwa*. 06:18:15 PM

Motherfucking flag's four stars: Fort Dearborn, the Great Fire, the World's Columbian Exposition, and the Century of fucking Progress. 06:26:38 PM

Fuck studying for this motherfucking testimony. Axelrod's back with pizza and beer. Your Honor, it's time to fucking drink. 06:32:23 PM

Tuesday, December 14, 2010

Motherfucking six fucking degrees? Fuck this motherfucking bullshit. 07:32:44 AM

I went out to grab the paper and now my motherfucking balls are frozen to my motherfucking leg. 07:52:30 AM

Axelrod's outside with a hair dryer trying to unfreeze the fucking fuel line on his Civic. He promises we'll be at City Hall by nine. 08:19:16 AM

And the Civic won't fucking start. Axelrod, Carl, and I are riding the motherfucking bus. Fucking perfect. 08:41:41 AM

Frozen balls, riding the bus, and giving fucking testimony to 25 motherfucking assholes. A+ motherfucking day. 08:45:46 AM

This residency hearing was a rather unique setup: Any petitioner was allowed to question Emanuel. About anything. As a result, Emanuel didn't just answer questions about his residency but about the 1993 shootout in Waco, Texas; whether his job as chief of staff was "a 9 to 5"; whether he was financing his campaign; and whether he was a member of the Communist Party. The media reports, which used the word "circus" more than you'd think, included lines like this, from the *Chicago Tribune*'s live blog: "An activist known as Queen

Sister Georzetta Deloney, who wore a golden headpiece, offered more statements than questions." (Deloney at one point referred to a coat in Emanuel's storage space as a "technicolor dreamcoat." Emanuel replied: "I'd like the record to show it's not a technicolor dreamcoat. It's an imitation leather jacket my grandfather gave my father.") In all, the petitioners, which included election lawyers and regular citizens, kept Emanuel on the stand for eleven hours.

Someone keep count on how many times I "itch" my eye with my middle finger during testimony today. I bet 352 fucking times. 08:57:43 AM

In the bathroom at City Hall, trying to dethaw my ballsack at the hand dryer and Dock fucking Walls walks in. Fuck this day. 09:12:35 AM

A former aide to Harold Washington, William "Dock" Walls had run for mayor of Chicago repeatedly and was the only candidate to openly challenge Emanuel's residency. His lawyer, Andrew Finko, was one of the questioners at the hearing.

■ ■ ■

Well here goes motherfucking nothing. 10:00:13 AM

I swear to god, if Axelrod shows up at lunch break with fucking Subway, I'm going to completely lose my motherfucking shit. 10:27:02 AM

These questions are awesome. I'll take "Fuck You in the Motherfucking Armpit" for $500, please. 11:59:06 AM

I am going to drink more alcohol than you can ever possibly imagine when this motherfucking godforsaken shitstorm of a day is over. 02:12:10 PM

Five hours of this testimony and I've come to one conclusion: people are motherfucking assholes. 02:57:38 PM

To each one of you motherfuckers asking me questions: in three months I'll be mayor and you'll still just be some dumb motherfucker. 03:19:23 PM

Some dumb motherfucker . . . that I hate. Hope you enjoy today. 03:20:21 PM

Well, that's over. Motherfucking fucking motherfuck. 05:08:06 PM

It actually wasn't over. The hearing wrapped up at almost 9 pm.

Off to eat a steak the size of my head, then go home and punch a fucking mirror until my knuckles are motherfucking pulp. 05:32:14 PM

Operation Clog Every Toilet

Wednesday, December 15, 2010

Holy motherfucking mother of god, I need to swim in a goddamn fucking ocean of motherfucking coffee right fucking now. 07:24:45 AM

Carl the Intern makes this breakfast that's a pancake wrapped around a hard-boiled egg with a sausage stuck through it. Fucking incredible. 08:22:39 AM

Sent Carl the Intern over to City Hall. Operation "Clog Every Motherfucking Toilet in the Fucking Place" is under way. 09:47:31 AM

All water flows downhill. Those motherfuckers in the basement hearing room will be swimming in shit by 1 pm. Motherfucking payback. 10:13:43 AM

Axelrod's watching video of my hearing and listening to the "Tron" soundtrack. Looked at me in tears: "Life's easier in the Grid." 10:43:04 AM

■ ■ ■

I don't even know how this is fucking possible, but somehow Carl the Intern is stuck in the sewer pipes below City Hall. Fuck. 02:46:44 PM

■ ■ ■

Fuck, now Axelrod is fucking stuck under City Hall too. 03:49:20 PM

■ ■ ■

Fucking goddamn motherfuck. I'm fucking stuck down here too. All three of us, in the fucking sewers below City Hall. 04:53:21 PM

■ ■ ■

Someone make a note to remind me that when I'm mayor, the first order of business is to fix the fucking City Hall sewer access door latch. 05:06:53 PM

Downside: looks like we'll be down here for a while. Upside: Axelrod's got like 30 fucking Slim Jims in his fanny pack. 05:20:44 PM

Emptied our pockets: 25 Slim Jims, four packs of NutraSweet, three pens, and a fucking pocket guide to Midwestern water fowl. So we're good. 05:38:01 PM

It's actually kind of beautiful down here. Quiet, except for the sound of water flowing. You forget where you are—until someone flushes. 05:44:32 PM

■ ■ ■

Forced open a door and discovered Jane Byrne's secret fucking office. A desk, a wet box of smokes, and a stack of Playgirls from 1981. 06:57:20 PM

Jane Byrne was mayor of Chicago from 1979 to 1983.

Ate the last Slim Jim. Fucking fuck motherfuck. 07:31:42 PM

It takes them less than two hours to eat 25 Slim Jims.

The plan: we're going to ride Jane Byrne's sex dungeon door down this river of shit and on to motherfucking freedom. 07:42:47 PM

■ ■ ■

Freedom! We're floating down the middle of Lake Calumet. There's snow in the air and the stench of shit on our clothes. Magical. 09:19:21 PM

Lake Calumet, located on the city's far South Side, is a heavily industrialized lake. Due to the pollution from decades of industry, significant parts of the Lake Calumet area were declared a Superfund cleanup site in 2010.

Movie Night (part two)

Thursday, December 16, 2010

Holy fuck: I've just woken up with a motherfucking raging case of pinkeye. I want to claw my eyeballs out of my fucking head. 07:36:14 AM

Axelrod too: he's sitting in the kitchen with a bag of frozen peas on his motherfucking eyes, moaning. 07:41:49 AM

Turns out Axelrod's mostly moaning about having to wait 16 hours until the midnight opening of motherfucking "Tron." 07:53:30 AM

Tron: Legacy, which came out that day, is the sequel to the 1982 movie about a man who gets digitized into a mainframe computer. As a nerdy eight-year-old I found it, seriously, the greatest movie I'd ever seen.

That also explains why he's wearing a light-up suit. 07:54:24 AM

Jesus fucking Christ, Carl the Intern just walked in. His eyes look like they're having their fucking period. 08:00:19 AM

Axelrod just showed me the "Tron" trailer. Holy fucking fuck, grown fucking adults watch that bullshit? 08:19:09 AM

■ ■ ■

If Axelrod doesn't stop talking about "Tron" soon, I'm going to download his fucking ass into a computer for the next 25 years. 11:39:57 AM

Carl brought Peppermint Mochas and Axelrod drank his, but he's lactose intolerant. Now there's puke down the front of his blinky "Tron" suit. 03:20:17 PM

Axelrod just threw his light-up "Tron" frisbee through the front window. Fuck. 05:36:07 PM

■ ■ ■

Standing in this line for "Tron" with Axelrod and Carl the Intern. These fucking light-up body suits are both demeaning and fucking cold. 08:26:07 PM

Meeks just rolled up to the theater in like a fucking for-real lightcycle. His red suit looks amazing too. Fucking motherfuck. 08:51:48 PM

Carol Moseley Braun just pulled up with full-sized Master Control head fucking glowing on the back of a pickup. We look like fucking chumps. 09:47:22 PM

Gery Chico's just dressed like Gery Chico, but that's because he's seeing "Love and Other Drugs." Again. 10:01:19 PM

Sunshine Fucking Baseball

Friday, December 17, 2010

Motherfucking coffee. Sweet motherfucking relief. 08:15:23 AM

New slogan: "Don't fuck with a guy with a huge fucking crawlspace. Emanuel '11." 08:37:10 AM

One of the points brought up at the residency hearing was that Emanuel claimed to be storing a lot of personal items—including his wife's wedding dress and a jacket his grandfather gave him—in the basement of his house. However, the tenants testified that they saw no boxes in the basement. Emanuel said that this was because the boxes were in a crawlspace and, eventually, his lawyers produced photographic evidence of an enormous crawlspace under an extension Emanuel had put on the house. Calling it a "crawlspace" doesn't really do it justice. It is large enough to store dozens of boxes. The photographs of the crawlspace showed that it included a full-sized *New York Times* newspaper box—which, when you think of it, is both bad-ass and really weird.

■ ■ ■

Riding in the Civic to hook back up with Ernie Banks. Tonight we're going to fuck this town until it can't walk straight. 04:30:40 PM

Earlier in the day Rahm Emanuel had had breakfast with "Mr. Cub" Ernie Banks. Banks is a Chicago legend, having played every one of his 13 years as a professional baseball player for the Cubs, retiring in 1971. He is, by most accounts, incredibly nice.

Fuck this motherfucking week, it's motherfucking over. Friday night, bitches. 04:46:05 PM

Ernie Banks' plan: grab his bat, pick up a case of Old Style, and hit the empties through Halpin's front window. Mr. Motherfucking Cub. 05:06:41 PM

You haven't lived until you've driven around with Ernie Banks hanging out your window yelling, "You just got fucked by Mr. Cub!" 06:11:59 PM

■ ■ ■

Ernie Banks is standing in the middle of Ashland, taking swings at cars as they drive by. Seriously considering fucking leaving him here. 08:16:04 PM

OK, he's standing on the roof of a cop car, trying to knock the lights off it, yelling, "Sunshine fucking baseball!" We're out. 08:29:30 PM

Paperwork

Saturday, December 18, 2010

Motherfucking fuck this Saturday morning meeting in its motherfucking nostril. 08:57:18 AM

Plouffe faxed in a suggestion that we "extend an olive branch" to the other candidates. The only thing I'll extend is my motherfucking cock. 09:32:35 AM

■ ■ ■

I'm still stunned about the Don't Ask Don't Tell repeal. Figured the Senate was going to stuff it up its ass like they do everything else. 08:41:44 PM

The US Senate had just voted to repeal the Clinton-era "Don't Ask, Don't Tell" policy that regulated the service of gays and lesbians in the military.

That said, Carl the Intern is fucking thrilled. But he still has to wait two more years before he can enlist. 08:52:02 PM

It took two months, but Carl the Intern finally had a coherent age: he's 16. And gay.

Sunday, December 19, 2010

Christmas next weekend means fucking meetings all motherfucking day today. Fuck you, Jesus. 11:13:00 AM

I would rather be nailed to a motherfucking cross than sit through another five minutes of this fucking marketing presentation. 11:18:22 AM

■ ■ ■

Working on writing my last residency briefs for tomorrow. End with just "Fuck You," or "Fuck you, you fucking fucks"? 09:15:03 PM

Fuck this—going to bed. Just signed the papers: "Suck it out of my asshole. Yours, Rahm." 09:48:35 PM

Monday, December 20, 2010

The stereo in Axelrod's Civic broke over the summer. Now the radio he lugs around is stuck on the fucking Christmas songs station. Fuck. 09:41:19 AM

Turned in the last paperwork: Seventeen Xeroxes of my cock and three of my asshole. Plus my signature. Done. With. This. Shit. 10:00:23 AM

New Office

New office. Carl wired the fucking phones wrong, so the calls are for the curry place down the block. Axelrod's tandoori is amazing. Phew. 11:50:08 AM

■ ■ ■

Axelrod's been driving around delivering curry all day, so Carl and I have spent the day playing a fucking wicked game of foosball. 05:01:22 PM

Axelrod just called from "the weathercenter" (what the fucking fuck) to tell us that it's snowing. He pulled over to put snow tires on. 05:57:44 PM

I'm all for motherfucking winter safety, but Axelrod had better get here with the chicken tikka we ordered before kickoff. 06:37:45 PM

Motherfucking Chicago fucking Bears fucking football. Fuck yes. 08:17:45 PM

The Bears played the Minnesota Vikings.

Hey, Favre, welcome to motherfucking Chicago. 08:41:12 PM

Halftime and Axelrod's not back with our Chicken Tikka. Still has 15 deliveries to go. All Carl knows how to make are Hot Pockets. Fuck. 09:14:26 PM

Axelrod just called. The Civic spun out on Elston. With our fucking chicken. Fucking motherfuck these fucking football snacks. 09:59:07 PM

Axelrod got the Civic unstuck. Bring that motherfucking chicken home. 10:27:34 PM

Post-season, you glorious motherfucking motherfuckers. 10:40:24 PM

Axelrod just showed up. 39 seconds to enjoy this fucking chicken. 10:43:42 PM

Going to pound a beer and text Favre a picture of my dick. Bears fuck yes. 10:46:27 PM

The Bears won decisively, 40–14, clinching the NFC North division title.

Tuesday, December 21, 2010

Holy Jesus fucking Christ, I just threw my back out shoveling that 800-pound snow. Fuck fucking motherfuckers. 08:02:56 AM

Holy fucking fuck, I took way too many muscle relaxers for my back. I feel like Gumby. 12:07:42 PM

Spent the entire day flat on my back tripping on muscle relaxers and not giving a fuck about any fucking thing. It's been fucking glorious. 08:05:42 PM

Wednesday, December 22, 2010

Hey, Chico—bend the fuck over, you fucking shitbag. Welcome to the campaign. 08:44:48 AM

The *Chicago Tribune*'s lead story that day was "Gery Chico made millions from law firm that lobbies City Hall." The story explained that Chico's law firm, Chico & Nunes, "is a registered City Hall lobbyist for more than 40 companies."

Seriously, who the fuck releases their tax returns when they know they're filled with lobbying cash? You dumb fucking fuck. 08:50:54 AM

Nutcracking

Carl's stepmom just gave all of us tickets to the "Nutcracker Ballet" tonight. First off: what the fuck. Second off: should be me onstage. 03:14:49 PM

Fun fact about Rahm Emanuel: He used to be a dancer. A good one, by all accounts. Out of high school he was offered a scholarship to the

Joffrey Ballet School, Chicago's renowned dance company. He turned it down to attend Sarah Lawrence, where he continued to dance.

Busy day driving Axelrod's Civic by other candidates' offices, pelting them with snowballs and yelling "43 points, bitches!" 03:22:02 PM

The Chicago Retail Merchants Association had just released a poll that had Emanuel at 43%. His next closest competitor was Gery Chico at 11%, a 32% gap.

I'm going to be spending the next two hours figuring out what to wear to the ballet. Nothing is goddamn good enough for those people. 04:41:23 PM

Seriously, you try and try and try, and the Joffrey motherfucking Ballet just fucking judges you anyway. 05:02:20 PM

Axelrod just showed up dressed in a fucking tuxedo T-shirt. "Let's get this fun over with." 05:34:13 PM

I went with the straight black tux, tie, and shirt. Black Swan, motherfuckers. Let's do this fucking ballet. 06:34:08 PM

I'd never actually seen the film *Black Swan*, but it had been released earlier in December and was still garnering quite a bit of press.

Five minutes in, Axelrod's already fucking snoring. 07:05:35 PM

Who the fuck is playing Drosselmeyer? He needs to hang up the motherfucking tights. Amateur fucking hour. 07:17:07 PM

Seriously, Clara may as well just pull down her tutu and take a shit on the stage. Would be more elegant than her dancing. 07:29:59 PM

It's plié, dégagé, motherfucking balancé, you fucking cows. 07:39:51 PM

I would rather rim James Meeks' asshole than have to endure another minute watching the Mouse King waddle around. 07:52:29 PM

You call that a motherfucking sugar plum fairy? 08:09:28 PM

Back when I danced, the Joffrey Ballet meant something. Now it apparently means fat fucking fucks floundering around a stage. 09:52:48 PM

Now I know why they call it the "Nutcracker"—I feel like my nuts have been fucking cracked in goddamn half. Wake up, Axelrod, this shit is over. 09:54:55 PM

Eligible, Bitches

Thursday, December 23, 2010

ELIGIBLE. Choke on that, you motherfucking bitches. 06:31:58 AM

> The way ballot challenges work in Chicago is that the Chicago Board of Election Commissioners gets a recommendation from the hearing officer. The Board itself makes a final ruling that can then be appealed to the Circuit Court. The hearing officer for Emanuel's case, Joseph Morris, issued his ruling early in the morning—the original expectation had been that it would be released the day before.

Been drinking Irish coffees since two in the morning, celebrating this residency shit. Fuck all the motherfucking haters. 07:52:04 AM

All you motherfuckers can stick your motherfucking objections up your ass. RESIDENT, bitch. 08:36:06 AM

Those stupid fucking objectors had to submit their home addresses. Think they'll be getting a visit from the ghost of Christmas yet to come. 08:45:12 AM

■ ■ ■

Fuck yes two times, bitches. 11:56:36 AM

> The Board of Election reaffirmed the recommendation by Morris.

It's no Christmas fucking miracle, it's a Christmas fucking fact. As real as the motherfucking virgin birth. Believe! 12:20:34 PM

I feel like a new man. Sent a street boy to fetch the prize turkey. "What, the one as big as me?" No, dumbfuck, the tiny one. 12:54:58 PM

Major upside of this residency bullshit being over: I can stop being folksy at your motherfucking L stops. 03:43:16 PM

■ ■ ■

Hey Meeks, too bad your ass got sacked. 04:43:27 PM

> On the same day that Emanuel's residency was confirmed by the Chicago Board of Election, James Meeks announced that he was withdrawing from the mayoral race. Technically, it was the last day to withdraw.

Axelrod and I had a great James Meeks drinking game. Take a shot when he said stupid shit. Could fuck you up in seconds. 05:09:17 PM

Without Meeks, this race got even fucking boringer. I'm going to be fucking catatonic by motherfucking February. 05:18:20 PM

Last few hours to be like Meeks and get the fuck out of this race. Stay in and I will make the next two months of your life a living hell. 08:33:43 PM

What a Fucking Blockhead

Friday, December 24, 2010

Plouffe has us out here freezing our fucking asses off bell ringing on State Street. We have a bet going to see who raises the most. 10:07:07 AM

Right now, Axelrod, Carl the Intern, and I are getting fucking creamed by the motherfucking bucket drummer kids. Fuck this shit. 10:30:26 AM

Axelrod ducked into the bathroom and came out dressed as one of those silver robot guys. He's going to raise a fucking fortune. 11:56:53 AM

Axelrod must have 100 fucking people crowded around him. I need to step it up here. Sending Carl the Intern to the Christmas tree lot. 12:15:06 PM

Carl's back from the tree lot. He bought the shittiest tree ever. Hung one ornament and it bent. What a fucking blockhead. 12:40:55 PM

> The original plan was to do a whole Charlie Brown Christmas thing, with Axelrod giving the famous Linus speech. But this single Tweet felt a lot better. Summed up the whole show in 140 characters.

Goddamn it, that's it: I'm paying the fucking bucket-drummer kids $500 an hour to drum for me. Fuck you, Robot Axelrod. 01:14:24 PM

Final haul from bell ringing: Carl brought in $22.73; Robot Axelrod, $271.58; my drummer boys, $321.93. They cost $2k. Fucking Christmas. 05:16:16 PM

Saturday, December 25, 2010

Merry motherfucking Christmas, you stupid fucking fucks. 08:14:22 AM

■ ■ ■

The only thing open in this fucking city is a motherfucking CVS. Axelrod, Carl the Intern and I have been wandering the aisles for hours. 09:20:23 PM

I'm trying to convince Axelrod that we should buy a bottle of Nair and just fucking obliterate his mustache. 09:41:30 PM

We've loaded up our cart with every fucking "As Seen on TV" piece of shit they have here. Snuggies for motherfucking everyone. 09:45:10 PM

Bought every bottle of lube in the store and are going to coat Davis's office sidewalk with them. Slip and slide, motherfucker. 10:04:12 PM

After that, we're going to head home, do Benadryl shots, and play motherfucking Uno. Christmas fucking sucks. 10:09:23 PM

Sunday, December 26, 2010

Motherfucking Benadryl hangover. Fuck. 08:50:25 AM

Motherfuck this snow right in its motherfucking lake-effect ass. 09:05:04 AM

> Ten inches of lake-effect snow fell the day after Christmas. Lake-effect snow happens when cold winter air moves over warmer lake water. Typically, Northwest Indiana and Michigan get hammered by lake-effect snow, because the prevailing winds move west to east. But occasionally, near the shore, Chicago gets pummeled too.

Axelrod is a motherfucking parking-space shoveling artist. They should hang his fucking shovel in the Art Institute. 11:07:03 AM

He's marked his space with 14 lawn chairs, an ironing board, and a pyramid of milk crates. He'll fucking shank someone if they move them. 11:09:37 AM

Carl the Intern's stepmother just stopped by to drop off an extra pair of snowpants for him. She parked in Axelrod's space. Fuck. 11:34:05 AM

Axelrod just pulled up, jumped out of his car, and keyed "FUCK YOU IN THE ASS" into the hood of her Escalade. Shit. 11:38:17 AM

■ ■ ■

Hey, New York, you just got fucked by the motherfucking Chicago fucking Bears. 03:22:33 PM

> The Bears beat the New York Jets 38–34.

Who Really Gives a Fuck Week

Monday, December 27, 2010

Holy fucking fuck, someone get me a fucking cup of fucking coffee right fucking now. 08:36:32 AM

■ ■ ■

Off to the Millennium Park ice rink. I'm going to show some motherfuckers what the motherfucking Russian Splits are all about. 12:29:36 PM

■ ■ ■

This motherfucking cold weather makes me realize that Axelrod really needs to up his fucking knowledge of hot liquor drinks. 08:48:39 PM

Tuesday, December 28, 2010

Spent most of the night last night dumping buckets of water on Gery Chico's car. It's a motherfucking ice cube now. 10:18:02 AM

■ ■ ■

This time between Christmas and New Year's may as well be renamed "Who Really Gives a Fuck Week." 01:39:42 PM

■ ■ ■

Whoever is advising Davis is doing a motherfucking incredible job. Keep up the fucking fantastic work. 08:26:43 PM

> It was reported that former President Bill Clinton would campaign for Emanuel in January. Danny Davis went on newscasts decrying the decision. He told ABC 7 that "There has been tremendous affinity between the African-American community and the Clintons. I would hope to continue that track. I just simply hope that the President would be neutral."

Wednesday, December 29, 2010

Jesus fucking Christ, there is not enough motherfucking coffee in the whole fucking world this morning. 07:33:27 AM

We're bringing every motherfucking distant fucking relative of Bill Clinton to town, just to make Davis's head explode. 08:09:20 AM

If your last name even rhymes with Clinton, you're getting a call from Carl the Intern and a ticket to Chicago on the fucking Greyhound. 08:11:21 AM

We've got a guy named Phil Clinton and another guy named Bill Kimpton on the motherfucking Megabus as we speak. 08:29:30 AM

Braun, if you want to get in on this bullshit too, know that we've got Hillary Rodman-Klinkton on motherfucking speed dial. 08:32:38 AM

■ ■ ■

Holy fuck! It's actually above motherfucking freezing outside right now. Axelrod's in his fucking Speedo. 11:18:56 AM

Motherfucking melt this fucking snow, you motherfucking southerly breeze. 12:55:21 PM

If it gets above 40 tomorrow, I'm putting on a fireproof suit, jumping in a spaceship, and flying up to fuck the glorious sun. 01:29:32 PM

Kicking

Thursday, December 30, 2010

Fuck these Angry Birds right in their motherfucking feathered fucking vents. 08:04:32 AM

> Angry Birds, a game where you "throw" birds in an attempt to knock down structures and kill green pigs (really), had become a massive, mainstream gaming hit over the Christmas season.

Carl the Intern left his iPod Touch here and I've been up most of the fucking night playing it. It is motherfucking maddening. 08:10:34 AM

■ ■ ■

They give you these motherfucking exploding fucking birds, but then they surround the goddamn pigs with fucking stone blocks? Fuck! 10:16:26 AM

■ ■ ■

These motherfucking egg-dropping birds are fucking driving me fucking crazy. How the fucking fuck am I supposed to control this shit? 11:41:47 AM

■ ■ ■

Fuck this bullshit. Fuck this bullshit. Fuck this bullshit. Fuck this motherfucking green pig fortress bullshit. 12:35:02 PM

■ ■ ■

These fucking boomerang birds might as well be flying up my own motherfucking asshole for all the fucking help they are. 01:52:09 PM

■ ■ ■

These giant bowling ball-red birds would be motherfucking amazing if this whole game wasn't fucking me in the ass right now. 03:09:36 PM

■ ■ ■

How many fucking levels are in this motherfucking game? Eight-fucking-thousand? Fuck. 04:16:51 PM

■ ■ ■

I've been awake since 7:45 yesterday morning, and have been playing Angry Birds for the last 19 hours. I fucking hate everything. 05:25:18 PM

All I want right now is a motherfucking cheeseburger and to claw my goddamn eyes out. Instead I'm fucking flinging these fucking birds. 05:29:04 PM

■ ■ ■

Axelrod just stormed into my room, stomped on the iPod, left and locked the door. He left a bucket behind—the fuck is that for? 06:30:20 PM

■ ■ ■

Axelrod and Carl are sitting outside my door, saying, "We're doing this because we love you." Fuck them. I NEED MY MOTHERFUCKING BIRDS. 09:46:57 PM

Also, I really need them to come and empty my motherfucking bucket. Because that shit is fucking full to the top. 09:47:37 PM

■ ■ ■

birds . . . birds . . . birds . . . .bird . . . fuck. 11:28:59 PM   •

2011 Is My Goddamn Year

Friday, December 31, 2010

Motherfucking sweet fucking coffee, there is nothing in the world better than you. Except maybe liquor. Or vaginas. 08:14:18 AM

New Year's Eve, I am going to bust you the fuck open. 09:23:14 AM

Axelrod's walking around wearing these fucking huge 2011 novelty glasses and his Speedo. "I'm the Baby fucking New Year." 10:38:40 AM

■ ■ ■

Carl the Intern's stepmom is out of town, so the party's at his house tonight, you motherfuckers. 12:45:49 PM

Penny Pritzker just called. Her chef is mixing up some homebrew Four Loko for the party tonight. Motherfucking double caffeine. 02:05:43 PM

Ernie Banks keeps popping up on the Caller ID, but we're all trying to avoid him. Motherfucker cannot hold his liquor. 02:13:36 PM

Oh fuck: "Hey you stupid fucking asshole, guess who flew into town?" It's Ari. He's here. 02:16:57 PM

Ari brought guests: Kanye West, three Victoria's Secret models he calls "the underpants twins," and Helen Mirren. Helen's already **drunk.** 03:35:19 PM

Kanye brought his green bean casserole. Again. "I brought it because it's fucking delicious." 03:39:08 PM

Carl's starting to get nervous about hosting the party. Doesn't help that Helen Mirren keeps trying to give him a backrub. "Jusht relacsh." 03:55:27 PM

Samurai Mike Singletary just called to find out if it's OK if he brings a dessert instead of a side salad. Fuck. 04:06:40 PM

Vince Vaughn just called to say he couldn't make it. Which is weird, because he wasn't invited, because he's a boring motherfucker. 04:13:48 PM

Vaughn grew up in the wealthy Chicago suburb of Lake Forest and is a die-hard Cubs fan.

Jeff Tweedy brought Pictionary. This party is going to get fucking insane. New Year's motherfucking Eve. 04:45:51 PM

Jeff Tweedy is the frontman for Chicago alt-country band Wilco. Rahm Emanuel is a huge fan.

Holy fucking fuck: Jane motherfucking Byrne just showed up. "This isn't a goddamn endorsement, kid; I just need to party." 05:53:46 PM

■ ■ ■

NUMBER ONE ON THE MOTHERFUCKING BALLOT, BITCHES.
07:36:51 PM

On New Year's Eve, Danny Davis, who had held the number-one spot on the ballot (Emanuel was number two), announced that he was dropping out of the mayoral race. Carol Moseley Braun was officially declared the "consensus candidate" for the African-American community.

Danny Davis just showed up. "Fuck this mayoral shit, I'm here to party!" He's doing body shots off Helen Mirren. Fuck yes. 08:01:17 PM

It turns out Danny Davis is fucking awesome. He and Tweedy are singing "Islands in the Stream" together on the karaoke machine.
09:24:34 PM

Also: Davis makes a fucking amazing drink called "The Leviathan." It's vodka, whiskey, strawberry yogurt, and peppermint schnapps.
09:32:10 PM

Kanye and Nobel Laureate Dale Mortensen have been playing beer pong against the Underpants Twins for like two fucking hours.
10:10:28 PM

> Mortensen is an economics professor at Northwestern University, who won the Nobel Prize in 2010 for "analysis of markets with search frictions," whatever that means.

Motherfuck: Ari just lit Carl's stepmom's underwear drawer on fire.
10:12:12 PM

Helen Mirren's fired up the motherfucking grill on the balcony. "Whip out your meat and I'll grill that shit." 10:37:34 PM

Penny just showed up with her homebrew Four Loko. Davis is downing the tropical fucking punch flavor. Watch the fuck out.
10:44:15 PM

Saturday, January 1, 2011

Happy New Year, you stupid motherfuckers. 2011 is my goddamn year. But I'll let you borrow it from time to time. 12:03:20 AM

Holy fuck. Apparently 2011 is going to start with a hangover the size of the motherfucking Sears Tower. 09:25:19 AM

Thank fucking god: Carl's got coffee going and Kanye's making eggs for everyone. "My bacon scrambler is fucking incredible."
09:42:04 AM

■ ■ ■

Jesus fucking Christ: Nobody can get Danny Davis to leave. He's just fucking lying around on the couch watching cartoons. 06:07:05 PM

Sunday, January 2, 2011

Need. More. Motherfucking. Coffee. 08:31:53 AM

■ ■ ■

We are swimming in motherfucking chicken wings over here. This fucking Bears game is fucking on. 03:34:06 PM

Someone wake me up when they start playing fucking football. 03:58:10 PM

This boring fucking game can suck on my motherfucking nuts. 05:27:51 PM

Axelrod just about choked to death on a chicken wing after that motherfucking Packers touchdown. Fuck. 05:32:20 PM

Fuck the motherfucking Green Bay fucking Packers. 06:06:23 PM

> The Bears lost to the Green Bay Packers 10–3, which allowed the Packers to move on to the post-season.

Monday, January 3, 2011

All-day meeting and someone ate all the motherfucking crullers? Fuck this shit. 07:53:16 AM

Main point of discussion: how little of a fuck do we give about Braun? Axelrod says a cock's-length. I say a twat's-hair. 08:22:35 AM

New slogan: "Because this list of opponents keeps getting shittier: Emanuel '11." 04:17:37 PM

Tax Returns

Tuesday, January 4, 2011

The best part of the next six weeks is going to be watching Carol Moseley Braun slowly fucking self-destruct. 09:41:31 AM

When asked that morning if she would release her tax returns, Braun responded that she wouldn't, "Because I don't want to." The local media went berserk.

Just for fucking fun, I'm going to release my tax returns dating all the way back to motherfucking Arby's. 09:42:22 AM

Emanuel worked at Arby's when he was in high school.

■ ■ ■

Carl the Intern's at the Circuit Court with three pounds of my shit in ziplock bags. He's tossing 'em if the verdict comes in wrong. 10:06:12 AM

The Chicago Board of Elections decision on Emanuel's residency was appealed up to the Cook County Circuit Court, which announced that a ruling would be issued that day.

Driving in Axelrod's Civic. He had to pull over because "I'll Be There" came on. We'll be here for an hour while he cries. 12:18:05 PM

Let's be honest: Axelrod's not alone—I still well up when I hear "I'll Be There" by the Jackson 5.

RESIDENT THREE TIMES, BITCHES. 01:24:51 PM

And the ruling was in: Circuit Court Associate Judge Mark Ballard ruled that Emanuel met the residency requirements and could stay on the ballot.

You motherfuckers want to appeal this shit, go right the fuck ahead. We're on the motherfucking winning streak to beat. 01:42:34 PM

We're taking this motherfucking winning streak to the motherfucking boats. Those fucking nickel slots won't know what fucking hit 'em. 01:56:03 PM

■ ■ ■

Won $78.35 at the boats. Going to convert it all to quarters and cram each one up Burt Odelson's motherfucking urethra. 04:28:39 PM

Burt Odelson is a prominent Chicago election lawyer and was the lead attorney in the residency battle.

■ ■ ■

I'm so excited to read Braun's tax returns tomorrow that I feel like a motherfucking kid on fucking Christmas goddamn Eve. 07:45:47 PM

In a single-day reversal, Carol Moseley Braun announced that she would in fact release her tax returns in the morning.

Wednesday, January 5, 2011

Fucking goddamn motherfuck, I fucking need fucking coffee so motherfucking badly. 08:26:29 AM

Staging dramatic readings of Carol Moseley Braun's tax returns. Carl's playing the part of "What the fuck were you thinking?" 10:19:11 AM

The headline in the *Chicago Tribune* really said it all: "Carol Moseley Braun tax returns reveal shaky financial state."

Axelrod is in tears, he's laughing so fucking hard. "Do the part again where she made no money in 2009." 10:44:03 AM

Moseley Braun's only reported income in 2009—$15,954—was from public pensions.

Moving Day-ley

Been trying to think of something nice to say about Bill Daley: his bald head is fucking magnificent. Too bad about the rest of him. 04:29:14 PM

Bill Daley, the brother of Mayor Richard M. Daley, was announced as President Obama's new chief of staff, filling the slot Emanuel vacated.

Thursday, January 6, 2011

Axelrod just made breakfast. "I call it the Bacon Palace." My heart's going to fucking stop. 07:43:11 AM

• • •

Great. Now Bill Daley keeps calling. He wants me to help pack his motherfucking U-Haul. Fuck. 01:31:03 PM

"Rahm, it's Bill. Since I've got your old job, and you're getting my brother's old job, I think you can help move these book boxes." Fuck. 02:52:15 PM

Fourteen motherfucking voice mails like that. I'm tossing this fucking phone in the lake. 02:53:28 PM

Friday, January 7, 2011

In Axelrod's Civic on the way over to Bill Daley's place to help him move. He'd better have motherfucking donuts. 07:55:33 AM

• • •

Daley moved some couch cushions, then started taking fucking calls. "I've gotta get this. Can you move that cast-iron stove?" 09:20:30 AM

Bill motherfucking Daley must have a thousand fucking book boxes. My fucking back is going to be so fucking fucked. 09:41:31 AM

Guess who just had to "duck out on Presidential business," right as we were starting to move his fucking free weights? 10:06:53 AM

Daley's fucking sea-glass collection has to have each fucking piece individually fucking wrapped, first in tissue, then in bubble wrap. 11:46:29 AM

Motherfuck. Bill just came in and had a shitfit because it was supposed to be two motherfucking layers of tissue. Rewrapping now. 12:16:42 PM

Daley's got all his clothes packed in giant motherfucking steamer trunks, like he's setting sail on the motherfucking Titanic. 01:31:52 PM

This motherfucking piano is not going to fit in the motherfucking truck. 02:00:13 PM

We've had to repack this motherfucking truck twice. And the whole fucking time, Bill has been on his fucking phone.
05:04:52 PM

He keeps giving me this "You know how it goes" shrug. And I keep giving him a "Fuck you, you fucking fuck" glare right back.
05:07:09 PM

Fuck all this fucking shit. It's Friday motherfucking night. Let's fucking go. 05:37:06 PM

Saturday, January 8, 2011

Holy fucking fuck. I'm sitting in this goddamn massage chair all fucking day. Fuck you if you think I'm moving an inch. 08:39:05 AM

Motherfuck these tea party fuckholes. For fucking real.
04:37:32 PM

> This not particularly artful Tweet was @MayorEmanuel's only reaction to the Gabrielle Giffords shooting. Going further didn't feel appropriate.

Sunday, January 9, 2011

Axelrod plays a game called "bagel king," where you toss a bagel at his finger. If it lands on it, he eats the bagel. He's eaten fucking eight. 09:53:44 AM

■ ■ ■

Jesus fucking Christ. I have been locked in a walk-in meat cooler most of the motherfucking day. My cock is frozen fucking solid.
05:06:06 PM

I'm not even going to dignify how it fucking happened, but fuck me if I'm ever helping Axelrod cook a roast again. 05:09:58 PM

Monday, January 10, 2011

Jesus fucking Christ, waiting for this fucking coffee to brew might just motherfucking kill me. 07:48:55 AM

Certainly Crain's Chicago motherfucking Business has more to write about than fucking me. Don't the Groupon guys need their diapers changed? 08:02:24 AM

> This was a reaction to the first story written about @MayorEmanuel, "Rahm Emanuel, social media boost campaign humor in Chicago," published in *Crain's Chicago Business*. In it the real Rahm admitted to knowing about the account and said, "I think it's hilarious." It was, quite honestly, a story that let me exhale for the first time in months. It would also spawn dozens more stories about the account.

You Just Got Hamboned

Fucking Christ, Axelrod found a puppy underneath the L tracks today. He named him "Hambone" and has been talking in fucking baby talk since. 01:49:01 PM

This entire afternoon meeting has been taken up by Axelrod talking like he's the fucking puppy. 03:28:07 PM

That said, Hambone is fucking sharp. Really good debate advice. Someone get him a fucking Scooby Snack. 03:32:10 PM

Turns out Hambone is a motherfucking shitting machine. Heading out to "inaugurate" Chico's new offices. 05:33:43 PM

Hey, Chico, you just got motherfucking Hamboned. 06:13:56 PM

Tuesday, January 11, 2011

Motherfucking mother of god, whoever the fuck thought snow was a good idea today is fucking dead to me. 07:33:04 AM

> Chicago got five inches of snow on January 11.

Great. This fucking puppy is scared of the motherfucking snow. He's pissed all over the floor. Hambone sleeps in the fucking Civic tonight. 07:46:21 AM

Winter Games

Fuck lunch, we're going motherfucking sledding. Cricket Hill, bitches! 12:07:27 PM

Axelrod is a mustachioed bullet streaking down the side of that fucking hill. Zoo-fucking-oom. 12:27:16 PM

Carl the Intern's trying to go down standing up, but he keeps fucking falling off backwards. He's going to have a concussion. 12:30:11 PM

Me, I've fucking puked twice from going down spinnies on a motherfucking disc. Walking up for round fucking three. 12:31:00 PM

Axelrod's sledding outfit is one of the leftover luge suits from the Chicago 2016 Olympics photo shoot. Helmet and all. 12:36:32 PM

> One of Mayor Daley's missteps at the end of his term was making an expensive (and failed) bid for the 2016 Olympics. It included billboards and ads featuring heroic shots of athletes. Because it was the Summer Olympics, there wouldn't have been luge suits, but the image was too good to pass up.

When Axelrod gets to the bottom, he jumps off the sled, holds his hands straight over his head, and yells "STUCK THE FUCKING LANDING!" 12:41:32 PM

Jesus fucking Christ, I got half the fucking hill's worth of snow down my snowpants on that last run. 12:48:08 PM

Last sledding run is a pile-on: Axelrod on the bottom, then Carl, then me, with motherfucking Hambone barking away on top. 01:03:21 PM

We fucked that sledding hill so hard it's not going to walk straight for a week. 01:07:10 PM

Wednesday, January 12, 2011

Jesus fucking Christ, who replaced the Illinois statehouse with politicians with actual fucking balls? 08:39:32 AM

Normally in Springfield everyone's too busy shitting themselves to actually get anything fucking done. What fucking happened? 08:51:41 AM

> The State of Illinois was, and still is, in a massive budget deficit of at least $13 billion (second only to California's $25 billion). While many states were, and are, attempting to balance budgets only by cutting services, the Illinois legislature actually voted on January 12 to raise taxes to begin chipping away at the debt.

Axelrod is making four middle-finger ice sculptures to put in front of Braun's house. One for every fucking mortgage she has. 10:32:20 AM

> Another detail from the tax returns: Moseley Braun had four mortgages on her home in the Hyde Park neighborhood.

Rabbi Lopatin stopped by. He's got a sock full of batteries that is happy to explain to anyone the meaning of "blood libel." 10:45:33 AM

> Rabbi Asher Lopatin is the head of Chicago's Anshe Sholom B'nai Israel Congregation, Emanuel's hometown synagogue. I highly doubt he walks around with socks full of batteries, though the statement by Sarah Palin in the wake of the Gabrielle Giffords shooting, that "journalists and pundits should not manufacture a blood libel that serves only to incite the very hatred and violence they purport to condemn," might have tested his resolve.

■ ■ ■

Supposed to read position statements, but instead spent the last three hours listening to that motherfucking Kanye record. 03:11:03 PM

Plouffe faxed over a list of all the motherfucking "mayoral forums" coming up. I would rather shoot my left ball off than go to them all. 05:41:46 PM

Thursday, January 13, 2011

Motherfuck, this is a fucking hot cup of fucking coffee. I think I just burned my motherfucking uvula. 08:17:05 AM

■ ■ ■

Pork chop sandwiches for lunch. Bone-in, bitches. 12:06:24 PM

The pork chop sandwiches from Jim's Original (so named because
Jim Stefanovic is credited with creating the original Maxwell Street–
style Polish sausage back in the 1930s) are truly to die for. A staple on
the near–South Side for decades, the stand was shut down when the
University of Illinois at Chicago, in 2001, took ownership of the land,
which included both Jim's and the site of the historic Maxwell Street
Market. "This is a screw deal by UIC and Mayor Daley," Steve Balkin,
vice president of the Maxwell Street Historic Preservation Coalition,
wrote at the time. "I hope everyone who ever wants to get an authentic
Maxwell Polish and can't—I hope they remember Mayor Daley as the
man who caused this culinary and cultural tragedy to occur." The city
ended up agreeing to move Jim's Original a few blocks east. Get the
pork chop sandwich, which is always served with the bone in.

■ ■ ■

**One day, I'm never going to step foot in another goddamn L stop
ever a-fucking-gain. Today is not that fucking day.** 05:10:39 PM

Jesus fucking Christ, let's get this hand-shaking over with.
05:22:38 PM

Top on My List of Bullshit
I Don't Want to Fucking Do

Friday, January 14, 2011

**Someone needs to carve a portrait of whoever invented coffee into
the side of a motherfucking mountain.** 07:42:49 AM

■ ■ ■

**Debate at the motherfucking Tribune offices this morning. Top on
my list of bullshit that I don't want to fucking do.** 10:58:06 AM

The *Chicago Tribune* hosted a morning mayoral debate in the
newspaper's editorial boardroom.

Good thing we're sitting around a table, because I have to squeeze my balls occasionally just to stay awake. Boring fucking motherfuckers. 11:00:58 AM

When Del Valle talks, I swear to fucking god it sounds like one of the teachers in a fucking "Charlie Brown" cartoon. Mwah wah waaah, wah-uh. 11:03:13 AM

> That's Miguel Del Valle, the city clerk for the City of Chicago. In this race, he ran to the left of the other candidates, and received strong support among the city's progressive community.

Hearing Braun talk about austerity budgets is like listening to a fat guy talk about fasting. Stick with what you fucking know. 11:08:53 AM

My next response might be to just bang my head on the table until it fucking bleeds. 11:11:05 AM

So Braun's plan to get us out of this budget crisis is apparently to pull a motherfucking unicorn out of her ass. 11:17:15 AM

The best part about this fucking debate is that Carl the Intern is hanging outside the window on a washing platform, mooning the ed board. 11:33:41 AM

Jesus fucking Christ, could these questions be more predictable? How about we just tell you assholes what you're going to ask next. 11:41:40 AM

By all means, let's take time to talk about a motherfucking children's fucking museum. That seems fucking useful. 11:43:35 AM

> Right after a Tweet about the predictability of the questions, the questioning shifted to the Chicago Children's Museum, which had been weighing a move out of the Navy Pier tourist trap and into a new location in Grant Park, just east of downtown Chicago. This seemingly left-field question was asked in part because, when Grant Park was founded in 1835, it was decreed that the park was "public ground forever to remain vacant of buildings"; as a result, a public debate broke out over whether the museum could move to that location.

The worst part about this debate is that Plouffe faxed over a list of words I couldn't say, including "dickweed" and "twatwaffle." Fuck. 11:46:16 AM

It took 45 fucking minutes to get to the parking meter deal. Fucking Axelrod wins the bet—I thought it would take three. 11:52:00 AM

How the fucking fuck did I miss 13 installments in the "I Spit on Your Grave" franchise? Well, now I know what Clinton and I will be doing. 12:06:55 PM

> In discussing violence in the media, Braun referred to "I Spit on Your Grave Part 13," which does not exist. *I Spit on Your Grave* is a rape-revenge horror movie originally released in 1978 with the title *Day of the Woman*. The title was changed when the film was rereleased in 1980, and it retained the new title when it was remade and released once again in 2010. The remake is, ostensibly, what Braun meant to refer to.

Wait just one fucking second. "I Spit on Your Grave" only came out in October. They made 13 more movies in three months? I call bullshit, Carol. 12:10:44 PM

Well that's a fucking let-down. There goes my motherfucking Monday night. Clinton's going to make us watch "Saw" again instead. 12:11:43 PM

Can I get a voucher to skip the next fucking debate? 12:22:19 PM

Now Carl the Intern is swinging by the window, flashing double birds. That kid's fucking going places. 12:29:15 PM

Apparently, these other fucking candidates won't be happy until I fuck a motherfucking Care Bear. 12:39:06 PM

> An extended back-and-forth in the debate centered around Emanuel's disposition: "The question is one of temperament," Braun said. "This is the city of big shoulders, and we're considered to be tough Grabowskis and all of that, but we're not mean-spirited and nasty."

Thank fucking Christ that's over. Now we need to figure out a way to get Carl the Intern down. He's fucking stuck up there. 12:56:59 PM

■ ■ ■

Five o'clock, bitches—punch the fuck out. It's motherfucking Friday fucking night. 04:58:54 PM

What the fucking fuck kind of name is "Reince Priebus"?
05:23:57 PM

The name of the newly appointed head of the Republican National Committee.

MOTHERFUCKING RED FUCKING ALERT: "Reince Priebus" is a motherfucking anagram for "Beer's Epic Ruin." 05:30:33 PM

Saturday, January 15, 2011

Climbing the motherfucking French toast mountain this morning. Tally fucking ho. 09:29:30 AM

■ ■ ■

Motherfucking shit fuckers. I just slammed my motherfucking finger stub in the fucking door of Axelrod's fucking Civic.
01:46:34 PM

Tailgating

Sunday, January 16, 2011

Up too motherfucking early this morning. Fuck this fucking bullshit.
08:51:57 AM

Heading down to tailgate at motherfucking Soldier Field. Axelrod's wearing his homemade Staley costume, rigged with a drinking tube. 09:22:13 AM

Staley Da Bear is the official mascot of the Chicago Bears. The crew was heading down to Soldier Field to watch the Bears play the Seattle Seahawks in the divisional round of the playoffs.

We tried to talk him out of it, but Carl the Intern is dressed as a Lovabull. He's going to be fucking cold. 09:26:58 AM

The Lovabulls are the cheerleaders for the Chicago Bulls.

My giant bottle of Jack costume is too tall to fit on the L. Fuck. If you see a huge bottle of whiskey walking down Milwaukee, that's me. 09:30:15 AM

Axelrod's drinking tube is capped with a funnel. Every block or so, he's stopping and yelling, "PUT IT IN THE FUCKING FUNNEL!!" 09:37:30 AM

Axelrod's leading the entire fucking South Lot in singing "Bear Down, Chicago Bears," except he's singing it as "Drink Up, Chicago Fans." 10:12:19 AM

Axelrod's doing fucking handsprings in his fucking Bear costume. 10:21:35 AM

I'm in my giant Jack bottle knocking people down Urlacher-style and yelling "YOU JUST GOT JACK'D." Then we do a fucking shot. 10:43:57 AM

Carl the Intern just did a routine to C+C Music Factory's "Gonna Make You Sweat" that brought this whole fucking parking lot to a standstill. 11:20:09 AM

You're looking at the motherfucking king of the South Lot keg stands, bitches. 12:00:15 PM

After all this, nobody's found a fucking ticket for the goddamn game except Carl. 12:03:25 PM

■ ■ ■

Motherfucking touch motherfucking down motherfuckers. 12:11:10 PM

Just five minutes into the game, the Bears scored.

Fuck yes you beautiful fucking team. 12:43:50 PM

And another touchdown at the end of the first quarter.

There's a rule that Seattle can just give the fuck up, right? 01:00:34 PM

Followed by a third, scored by the quarterback, Jay Cutler.

Motherfucking Jay fucking Cutler, ladies and fucking gentlemen.
01:01:38 PM

Axelrod's been doing a shot every time Seattle has had to punt.
And Bears touchdowns. And time-outs. And penalties. He's fucking
gone. 01:26:16 PM

Axelrod was putting on his Staley costume for half time, but all
he could manage was the head before he started fucking puking.
01:40:25 PM

I say we just have Cutler run it every fucking play. 02:02:23 PM

Hey Seattle, we're giving out free concussions all motherfucking
game. Just step right the fuck up. 02:06:45 PM

Mother-touching fuck-down! 02:15:30 PM

I fucking blacked out for a minute there. Who the fuck let Seattle
score? 02:43:09 PM

We're going to need a fucking wheelbarrow to get Axelrod home.
Can someone bring one by the South Lot? 02:54:58 PM

Green fucking Bay is fucking fucked. Let's just do this shit today.
03:25:45 PM

Chicago won the game, 35–24, advancing to the conference
championship to meet the Green Bay Packers once again.

Still in the South Lot. Axelrod won't fucking move. It's OK though.
My fucking Jack Daniel's bottle costume is surprisingly warm.
04:33:12 PM

Axelrod just sat bolt upright, said "THE GOLDEN GLOBES!"
and took off fucking running. Guess it's time to head home.
05:15:37 PM

The Big Bear Strikes Back

Monday, January 17, 2011

Motherfucking shopping list for Clinton's visit tomorrow: 6 lbs. of hamburger, 18 bottles of vodka, 100 yards of plastic sheeting. 09:40:16 AM

■ ■ ■

Spent the entire day getting ready for Clinton. Plastic sheeting is a goddamn bitch to attach to the ceiling. 05:01:14 PM

Tuesday, January 18, 2011

I'm going to need a motherfucking Clinton-sized coffee to get me through this bullshit today. 07:26:00 AM

> Bill Clinton came to Chicago to campaign for Emanuel. He held a public rally as well as a private fund-raiser that raised $250,000.

■ ■ ■

Stuck in this fucking slush-fest on the way to the airport to pick up Clinton. Axelrod's spun out the Civic three times already. 10:22:43 AM

Clinton's been shotgunning vodka the whole drive in from the airport. I think I can hear his liver fucking sobbing. 11:09:17 AM

It's been a while since I've hung out with Clinton. When did he start referring to himself as "The Big Bear" fucking exclusively? 11:12:08 AM

Clinton's up on stage, drinking straight from the bottle. Crowd is tossing money and panties. The Big Bear's still fucking got it. 11:35:17 AM

Holy fucking fuck: Clinton just asked, "Who's seen 'The Puppetry of the Penis'?" ABORT! ABORT! ABORT! 11:54:29 AM

Finally got Clinton off the fucking stage. "But I was about to show them 'The Flamingo'!" 12:16:46 PM

■ ■ ■

Got Clinton back to my place, where he announced, "The Big Bear's gotta hibernate," and immediately passed the fuck out. 03:14:26 PM

Clinton just woke up and announced, "The Big Bear's ready to meat wrestle. Where're the girls?" Fuck. I had hoped he'd stay asleep. 06:15:17 PM

God, I fucking hope we've got enough plastic sheeting. 06:17:07 PM

Here's the other thing: we don't actually have any fucking girls. Carl and Axelrod are going to do their best. 06:20:31 PM

Managed to distract Clinton with news about Joe fucking Lieberman's retirement. Good riddance, you fucking froggy-voiced fuck. 07:30:22 PM

> News broke that evening that Connecticut Senator Joe Lieberman would be retiring.

And he's passed out again. Tends to go like this all fucking night with the Big Bear. 07:54:31 PM

Clinton's up again. And he's crying. Giant fucking rivers of tears. This night is never going to fucking end. 09:35:39 PM

Clinton's smeared raw fucking hamburger all over himself and is sliding across the plastic-sheeted floor. "I'm the king of the world!" 10:34:01 PM

Axelrod managed to get Clinton into a fucking sleeper hold. Sweet dreams, Big Bear. Sweet Dreams. 10:56:39 PM

Wednesday, January 19, 2011

Woke up and Clinton's gone! His clothes and wallet are here. He's gonna fucking freeze out there. Come back, Big Bear! 08:28:15 AM

Axelrod's going to search, but Carl the Intern said his Civic will freeze before he reaches the first marker. "Then I'll see you in hell!" 08:30:51 AM

You'd think that one extended reference to the Hoth scene in *The Empire Strikes Back* (the same as on December 13) would be enough in a six-month-long work of satire. You'd have thought wrong.

Axelrod found him, facedown in a snow bank muttering something about Ben Bernanke. Just "Ben . . . Ben . . . Ben . . ." over and over. The fuck? 09:16:56 AM

Ben *Bernanke* is the chairman of the Federal Reserve. Ben *Kenobi* is a strange old hermit who lives out beyond the Dune Sea and turns out to be the last of the Jedi Knights.

Axelrod cut open the back seat of his Civic—"I thought they smelled bad on the outside"—and stuffed Clinton inside to keep him warm. 09:21:46 AM

Now they're back, and Carl the Intern's filling this big-ass tube with hot water. Sticking Clinton in there to warm him the fuck up. 09:25:58 AM

Clinton looks strong enough to pull the ears off a motherfucking gundark. Axelrod says, "That's two you owe me, Big Bear." 10:04:28 AM

Now Axelrod and Carl the Intern are arguing and Hambone starts barking like crazy. Axelrod spins around and says, "Bark it up, fuzzball." 10:13:57 AM

And now Carl's planting a big kiss on Clinton, and he's just lying there, hands behind his head with a big shit-eating grin. What the fuck? 10:15:07 AM

We gotta get Clinton back to the airport now. I don't know how the fuck he's going to explain that big scar on his cheek to Hillary. 10:23:31 AM

Escape to Wisconsin

Motherfucking cock-chokers. How the fucking fuck is it only Wednesday? Spent all goddamn day thinking it was Thursday. 04:50:11 PM

Plan for tomorrow is to rent a truck, head to Costco, load up, and drive north to TP the living fuck out of Wisconsin. Go Bears. 08:58:37 PM

> With the NFC championship game vs. the Green Bay Packers coming up that weekend, the whole city was obsessed.

Thursday, January 20, 2011

Where can I buy a motherfucking vat of coffee? I don't want a fucking cup, I want an endless fucking vat. 07:34:35 AM

Hope you stocked up on toilet paper, because we just cleared Costco the fuck out. Wisconsin won't know what fucking hit it. 08:09:00 AM

Before the TPing, we're all getting tattoos. I'm getting "MOTHERFUCK GREEN BAY" across my shoulder blades. 08:45:14 AM

■ ■ ■

So I'm not saying we got stopped by the cops in Beloit, but I will say that I doubt we're going back to fucking Wisconsin any time soon. 03:22:42 PM

Also, if you need any motherfucking toilet paper we've probably got some extra. 03:28:58 PM

I've got 10.6 million fucking reasons the other motherfuckers are motherfucked. 03:53:36 PM

> The Emanuel campaign released its campaign finance details, revealing that Emanuel had raised $10.6 million since entering the race. He'd started with an additional $1.1 million in the bank from his congressional campaign, giving him $11.7 million. His closest competitor, Gery Chico, had raised $2.4 million in the same amount of time.

It's nice, after a day sitting in a truck on the side of I-90, to know that I have a giant fucking pile of money to roll the fuck around on. 04:12:03 PM

This tattoo is getting blood all over my tux for the Hu dinner. I hope nobody slaps me on the motherfucking back. 05:05:33 PM

Chinese President Hu Jintao visited Chicago for two days, his only stop other than Washington, DC, during this visit to the States. "It is a big deal," Mayor Daley told reporters in his unequaled style. "Big, big, big, big. Big deal."

Kissing the Pole

Friday, January 21, 2011

Fuck this motherfucking brutal fucking cold right in its frozen fucking asshole. 07:40:29 AM

Chicago descended into single-digit temperatures today, with 20 mile-an-hour wind gusts adding insult to injury.

We sent Carl the Intern out to get coffee, and he came back with three cups of motherfucking brown ice. Fuck this shit. 08:31:02 AM

The only thing getting me through this frozen fucking day is the fact that it's Friday. 09:54:31 AM

■ ■ ■

Axelrod, Carl the Intern, and I went out to kiss the flagpoles outside Soldier Field—you know, for fucking luck—and now we're stuck. 03:55:05 PM

Carl the Intern lined up some stupid fucking comedian to do a stupid fucking fund-raiser for me tonight. Because you know what we need? Money. 05:38:49 PM

Saturday Night Live's Andy Samberg—who impersonates Emanuel on the show—performed at a fund-raiser for him and shook hands at an L stop with him (while @MayorEmanuel was stuck to a pole).

Anyway, looks like I'm going to fucking miss it unless Mr. Fucking Funny shows up with some warm water to melt this frozen pole. 05:40:29 PM

Um. It's fucking dark and fucking cold out here. Uh. Help? 06:41:21 PM

■ ■ ■

Motherfucking motherfuck. Finally pulled my fucking lips off that fucking frozen flagpole. There's blood absolutely goddamn everywhere. 07:34:54 PM

Game On

Saturday, January 22, 2011

Oh, it did not just fucking snow again. I am so fucking over this motherfucking winter bullshit. 07:45:42 AM

Plouffe called. Our ad for tomorrow's game is a "no go." The fuck is wrong with an ad of Axelrod wiping his ass on a Packers helmet? 09:04:02 AM

■ ■ ■

Axelrod just got his tat finished: Calvin in a Bears uniform pissing on a block of cheese. "It's also 'cause I'm fucking lactose intolerant." 01:20:55 PM

Sunday, January 23, 2011

9 am Game Day. Let's get our motherfucking drink on. 09:14:23 AM

> The Bears-Packers rivalry has been going strong for 90 years. And seriously, people get crazy about it—the catchphrase used on newspaper boxes to hype the game was "Cold War," and it didn't feel all that inaccurate, either word. Also, in case you don't know, it's probably worth noting that Packers fans wear foam blocks of cheese on their heads, called "cheeseheads." Really.

Motherfucking hot-wing fryer fire! Holy fucking shit! 11:34:11 AM

So it turns out vodka isn't a very good fire extinguisher. Finally got it out with Axelrod's Bears Snuggie. In-fucking-flammable. 12:23:22 PM

Penny Pritzker just showed up with treats: shot glasses with $100 bills in them. "Who's getting a money shot?" 01:23:08 PM

Jeff Tweedy showed up with a giant plate of motherfucking brownies. "Game on, bitches." 01:54:58 PM

Doorbell. Holy fucking fuck, it's Ari. "You didn't think I'd miss this, did you, you stupid little shit?" 02:10:05 PM

I haven't even finished one of Tweedy's brownies yet, and the Packers are on the one? What the goddamn fuck? 02:11:11 PM

Fucking Christ fuck. What the fucking shit fucking fuck was that fucking bullshit? 02:12:46 PM

> The Green Bay Packers scored the first touchdown of the game.

Ari brought Spielberg, who is wearing a motherfucking cheesehead. We're holding Axelrod back right now. 02:15:42 PM

> Steven Spielberg donated $75,000 to Emanuel's mayoral campaign, but probably isn't a Cheesehead.

Christ, I am nowhere near fucking drunk enough for this motherfucking game. 02:21:43 PM

Kanye just called, in tears. "I can't watch this shit on my own. Can I drop by?" Fuck yes, Yeezy. Fuck yes. 02:33:52 PM

> A half-hour in, Green Bay was up by seven, Cutler had been sacked, and Green Bay quarterback Aaron Rodgers was tossing massive passes all over the place. It was painful.

Kanye showed up with the same fucking Motorola headsets the coaches have. We're all wearing them. We look fucking awesome. 02:45:19 PM

Fucking goddamn motherfuck. I'm going to go crawl under a motherfucking blanket now. 02:51:17 PM

> Another Green Bay TD.

Fucking goddamn motherfucking fuck. Fucking shit fucking fuck. Fucking fucktards need to fucking play this fucking game. 03:06:40 PM

Rogers ran the ball 25 yards on his own.

Kanye's a fucking mess right now. This game needs to turn around. 03:09:05 PM

Motherfucking interception, you bitches. Let's motherfucking do this shit. 03:23:29 PM

Motherfucking fucking motherfuck. 03:24:09 PM

Clearly, they didn't do this shit.

At this point, the only thing turning this motherfucking game around are some goddamn pizza rolls. Tweedy and Pritzker are making the run. 03:28:13 PM

My "MOTHERFUCK GREEN BAY" tattoo is going to look really fucking stupid if this game doesn't turn around. 03:35:30 PM

We finally got Spielberg to take off his cheesehead, but he's got a Packers do-rag on underneath it. What the fuck. 03:41:06 PM

Second fucking hot wings fire of the day. This shit just isn't getting any better, is it? 03:46:45 PM

Ari thought he could put the wings fire out by peeing on it. Turns out, that's not a great fucking idea. Carl the Intern's on a gauze run. 03:48:27 PM

Kanye's choking back fucking tears: "Cutler's knee injury is a nice match for my heart injury." 03:51:22 PM

It was announced that Cutler had hurt his knee and was out of the game.

MOTHERFUCKING BRIAN FUCKING URLACHER IS THE GREATEST FUCKING MAN IN MOTHERFUCKING HISTORY. 03:54:22 PM

Urlacher caught a Green Bay pass, sending back-up QB Todd Collins in.

I fucking hate fucking everything right fucking now. 03:56:55 PM

Collins threw an interception, it was overturned, but the Bears ended up punting.

Hey, Cutler: My knee hurt before I had to dance "Swan Lake" once. And you know what? I fucking danced the motherfuck out of it. Fuck you. 03:58:57 PM

Tweedy and Pritzker got back with the pizza rolls. Thank fucking god. Finally some good news. 04:05:55 PM

Carl the Intern is in seventh fucking heaven with Collins in. "It's like they're sending interns onto the field." He's fucking right. 04:13:00 PM

Jesus fucking Christ. They're just pulling people out of the fucking stands to be quarterback at this point, aren't they? 04:23:03 PM

Collins came out, and a third-string quarterback named Caleb Hanie was brought in.

CALEB FUCKING HANIE! YOU ARE A BEAUTIFUL FUCKING MAN! 04:28:46 PM

And the Bears finally scored, bringing the game to 14–7 Green Bay.

I HAVE NEVER FUCKING HEARD OF YOU EVER, BUT RIGHT NOW I LOVE YOU MORE THAN MY GODDAMN WIFE. 04:29:27 PM

Spielberg's smart fucking mouth isn't fucking mouthing so much now. Let's motherfucking do this. 04:38:49 PM

I will give Green Bay this: they have the most incredible display of man-tits I have ever fucking seen in my life. 04:42:30 PM

Fucking fuck motherfucking fuck. The fucking tubby guy just scored? Fucking fuck this fucking shit. 04:52:31 PM

Hanie threw an interception and the 338-pound B. J. Raji scored for Green Bay. 21–7 Green Bay.

Just sent Carl the Intern out for the biggest fuck-it bucket of chicken you have ever fucking seen. 04:54:53 PM

MOTHERFUCKING TOUCH FUCKING DOWN!!! HOLY FUCKING FUCK. WE CAN DO THIS FUCKING SHIT. BEAR THE FUCK DOWN. 04:57:05 PM

Another Bears TD brought it to 21–14 Green Bay.

I need to get one of those giant fucking sidelines jackets. They look so fucking bad-ass. 04:59:09 PM

Caleb Hanie. Be the ball. There is no motherfucking spoon. 05:04:49 PM

When Axelrod gets stressed out, he has to take a shit. He's been in the bathroom for most of this fucking quarter. 05:09:27 PM

Oh goddamn motherfuck. That's the fucking motherfucking game. I am going to get so fucking drunk I'll be hungover until Wednesday. 05:14:29 PM

The Bears lost to the Green Bay Packers, 21–14.

Fucking empty motherfucking emptiness. 05:16:20 PM

Kanye's got his vocoder set to a minor fucking key. We're all lost in this motherfucking world. Fuck. Fuck. Fuck. 05:17:57 PM

I'm not sure Axelrod's ever going to fucking get over this. 05:20:04 PM

Tweedy's post-game snack: the Hanie. A jalapeño popper stuffed inside a pizza roll. "Tastes like sadness." 05:47:56 PM

End of Days

Monday, January 24, 2011

Oh, coffee, you glorious motherfucking bean. 07:48:04 AM

■ ■ ■

Motherfucking shit fucking fuck shitters. What the fucking fuck motherfucking happened?! 12:18:35 PM

It was announced that the Illinois Appellate Court, in a 2–1 decision, had determined that Emanuel was not eligible to run for mayor, due to his residency. With that announcement, the Chicago Board of Election, which was to begin printing ballots that night, announced that it would print them without Emanuel's name. He was literally off the ballot.

OK, Carl the Intern makes a good point: appellate courts are for pussies. We're going to motherfucking Supreme this bullshit. 12:21:33 PM

My brain feels like it's on motherfucking fire. 12:23:22 PM

Throwing that chair through the window wasn't the best fucking decision in the world just now. Now we're fucked AND it's cold. 12:27:08 PM

I FUCKING HATE THE MOTHERFUCKING WORLD. WHO MOTHERFUCKING WANTS SOME? 12:31:10 PM

Jesus fucking Christ. I'm just lighting any fucking thing on fire right now. Just to feel fucking something. 12:32:20 PM

Holy fuck, we're so not getting the security deposit back on this motherfucking apartment. 12:36:23 PM

Axelrod's got his Bears helmet on and is just fucking punching gaping fucking holes in the walls with his motherfucking head. 12:38:30 PM

Holy fuck holy fuck holy fuck holy fuck holy fuck holy fuck holy fuck holy fuck holy fuck holy fuck holy fuck holy fuck holy fuck. 12:42:55 PM

Carl the Intern just tossed a lit mattress through the window. "We don't need no water, let the motherfucker burn." 12:46:00 PM

HOLY FUCK: Axelrod just flipped the Civic. This shit just got motherfucking realer than real. 12:50:25 PM

Every fucking thing in this motherfucking apartment is going through the front fucking window right fucking now. 12:53:44 PM

shit shit shit shit shit shit shit shit shit shit shit shit shit shit shit shit shit shit shit shit shit shit shit shit shit shit shit shit shit. 12:59:17 PM

Double birds to the motherfucking world. TO THE MOTHERFUCKING WORLD. 01:04:35 PM

They'll get to you too. They'll destroy you. They're untouchable, man . . . I'm so fucking exhausted I can't see straight. 01:09:54 PM

This is a direct quote from Joe Pesci in the film *JFK*.

motherfucking empty fucking emptiness. again. 01:14:32 PM

fucking why. 01:15:44 PM

motherfucking why. 01:16:05 PM

fuck. 01:16:29 PM

■ ■ ■

Fuck. I've been walking these streets at night. Just trying to get it right. 08:49:01 PM

Alone, cold, and singing the Guns N' Roses ballad "Patience."

It's hard to see with so many around. You know I don't like being stuck in a motherfucking crowd. 08:49:43 PM

And the fucking streets don't change but maybe the name. 08:50:42 PM

I ain't got time for this fucking game. 08:51:43 PM

It's nice, this fucking city, in the dark. The snow and the ice. The bridges. The water. It's quiet. I just need some fucking quiet. 08:56:03 PM

We trashed the apartment so fucking bad, there's nothing to go back to. 09:10:31 PM

Last I saw Carl the Intern and Axelrod, they were going to drive the Civic into City Hall. They're probably fucking locked up now. 09:11:19 PM

Now it's just me and Axelrod's little puppy Hambone. Against the motherfucking world. 09:15:48 PM

Found a spot under a bridge on Cortland. It's pretty here, and there's a hot air vent. This'll do. What a motherfucking fucked day. 09:26:35 PM

Quack Fucking Quack

Tuesday, January 25, 2011

Woke up to Hambone licking my face. Now we're tossing chunks of ice into the river. Big fucking splash. Scared the ducks. 08:05:54 AM

The river water is brown like coffee, but it sure doesn't taste like coffee. I think I miss coffee the motherfucking most. 09:15:33 AM

There's a duck along the river here who has a bill with a little dark spot on it, like a mustache. Named him Quaxelrod. Quack fucking quack. 10:10:41 AM

> Let's be transparent here: the original Tweet named the duck "Axelrod" but immediately after posting, I realized the joke should have been "Quaxelrod," and the name stuck with the very next Tweet. I'm changing this one for the book, dammit.

Me, Hambone and Quaxelrod found a pretty sturdy sheet of ice and we're going to fucking float down the river for a while. 10:22:55 AM

■ ■ ■

Quaxelrod just started quacking like crazy. It's foggy, but I can see someone else fucking floating toward us. 12:01:00 PM

It's Daley! Floating the other way. "You're a hard man to find, you know. Here's some bread for your duck. Shut him the fuck up." 12:03:29 PM

"First off, you're back on. I mean, for now. Probably forever. The Supremes are assfucks, but they're my assfucks." Daley's hands are HUGE. 12:08:20 PM

Emanuel was back on the ballot, at least temporarily. The Illinois Supreme Court agreed to hear the case and, in the meantime, issued a stay on printing the ballots without Emanuel's name on them.

"But, really man, pull yourself the fuck together. You're running for mayor. Of Chicago. People are going to fuck with you all the time." 12:09:20 PM

"You think when I wanted to close Meigs Field, and they told me no, that I went adrift? No. I fucking closed Meigs fucking Field." 12:10:40 PM

Chicago used to have a small business airport on the lake just east of downtown called Meigs Field. Daley had wanted to close the airport and turn it into a park since 1994. The Chicago Park District didn't renew the lease in 1996, and the city and the state began to fight over the fate of the airport in earnest at that point. All seemed to be solved in 2001, when the city and the state announced a deal to keep the airport open for 25 more years. A done deal? You'd think so, but the Senate didn't pass some federal legislation that was part of the deal, so it fell apart. And that's when Daley, in 2003, carved giant X's in the runways, stranding 16 planes, and Meigs Field was no more.

"You think when they started pissing on the parking meter sale that I fucking tucked tail? No, I sold off everyfuckingthing else too." 12:11:21 PM

The end of Daley's tenure was marked with attempts to privatize far more than the parking meters, including Midway Airport and major street festivals like the Taste of Chicago.

"Here's something my dad told me once: The role of the mayor is to be the guy that everyone takes a shit on. And then to shit on them back." 12:13:13 PM

"Except he didn't say 'everyone.' He said, 'Blacks, Jews, Poles, and Hippies,' but those were different times. Fucking substance is the same." 12:14:04 PM

Richard M. Daley's father, Richard J. Daley, was mayor of Chicago from 1955 to 1976. That's right, do the math: in the 56 years from 1955 to 2011, a Daley was mayor for 43 of them.

"So you're going to turn this ice floe around, pack up your pets, and run for the goddamn mayor of Chicago and you're going to win." 12:16:54 PM

"And once you've won, you're going to fuck with every last one of these motherfuckers until they wish they'd never even heard your name." 12:18:14 PM

"Now if you'll excuse me, I'm floating my way down to Chinatown right now for some dim sum." And Daley's gone again, into the fog. 12:19:00 PM

Fuck this noise. Quaxelrod? Hambone? We've got a motherfucking election to motherfucking win. Let's do this shit. 12:24:51 PM

■ ■ ■

Fifty-two motherfucking percent, you stupid fucking motherfuckers. Quaxelrod is so excited, he's molting. 04:58:33 PM

The Chicago Retail Merchants Association released an overnight poll showing Emanuel with 52%—conducted the day he was kicked off the ballot. It was the first poll to get him over 50%, which, if it followed through to actual votes, would mean that a runoff between the top two vote-getters would not be necessary. Quick background on the Chicago mayoral election: because there's essentially a nonexistent Republican Party in the city, there is no party-based primary system. Instead, all candidates run in a February election and, if nobody receives above 50% of the vote (50% + 1 to be precise), a runoff occurs between the top two candidates a month and a half later. At this point, among all of the candidates, the practical strategy was not to win, but to keep Emanuel below 50% and force a runoff.

State of Disunion

Found a hotel room for the night. Dropping some major campaign cash. Holiday Inn Express, bitches. Quaxelrod can use the pool. 05:39:23 PM

Don't know if Obama's going to use the draft of the speech I wrote before I left. If he opens with double fucking birds, it's mine. 06:12:18 PM

President Obama was giving his third State of the Union address, his first without Emanuel as chief of staff.

Jesus fucking Christ. I turn on the hotel TV and the first thing I have to see is Bill Daley's bald fucking head? Fuck. 08:03:48 PM

That's right, Obama, walk down that aisle, and bust people's chops. "You were looking a little scruffy." That fucking scruffy fuck. 08:08:44 PM

Obama said that to a newly shorn Senator Tom Coburn, a Republican from Oklahoma, as he made his way to the Speaker's podium.

I had a whole State of the Union drinking game lined up, then I decided just to drink fucking all of it to begin with. Whoo fucking hoo. 08:09:28 PM

Jesus Christ. Boehner's not even orange anymore. He's burnt fucking ochre. 08:10:56 PM

Newly appointed Speaker of the House, Republican John Boehner, sported a shockingly deep tan at the address.

It's two years of experience with this when I tell you: the key is to keep your motherfucking eyes locked on fucking Biden. 08:12:54 PM

OK, see, I wrote this part. It ends with "Fuck Bush in his motherfucking shriveled fucking asshole. First CEO president my ass." 08:19:59 PM

OK, he took it in a different direction. Quaxelrod thinks the "win the future" thing is a nice flourish. I think it's for the birds. 08:22:30 PM

I'm not saying that I flipped away for a bit, but I will tell you there is a motherfucking "I Didn't Know I Was Pregnant" marathon on. 08:32:12 PM

This is an actual TV show, and there actually was a marathon of it on that night.

Boehner's really going for the "asshole of the year" award, huh? Yeah, douchebag, don't clap for student fucking aid. 08:35:27 PM

Wait a second—SHE didn't know she was pregnant? How the fucking fuck did that happen? Oh shit, sorry. Flipping back. 08:38:30 PM

See, I wrote that part too. Except it was originally "Let's fix what fucking needs fixing, and then let's move the fuck forward." 08:47:35 PM

> The actual quote, about the battles around the health-care law, was "Instead of refighting the battles of the last two years, let's fix what needs fixing and let's move forward."

Do you think Boehner painted open eyes on his eyelids, and he's just back there fucking snoozing? Fucking CLAP, man. 08:49:19 PM

Yeah, maybe I'm fucking standing on my fucking hotel bed fucking cheering about getting rid of "frivolous lawsuits." Maybe now? In Illinois? 08:52:07 PM

> Obama was talking about medical malpractice reform, not election law in Illinois.

See, I'd told him to not mention Iraq or Afghanistan. "Nobody fucking remembers them. Don't fucking remind them." 08:58:21 PM

Wait, wait wait—SHE didn't know she was pregnant either? The fuck, people? 09:00:43 PM

OK, so I wrote this part too. Unless SOMEONE went and changed it again, it should end with him double-chopping his cock and saying "SUCK IT." 09:09:46 PM

God, thinking about those fucking Chilean miners still makes me motherfucking weep. Beautiful fucking people, stuck in a tiny fucking hole. 09:12:09 PM

> Obama mentioned the saga of the Chilean miners by talking about the Pennsylvania company that built the drill that helped saved them.

OK, maybe they moved the crotch chop to this part. Because it would be fucking perfect here. 09:12:55 PM

I thought the speech was pretty great. I mean, it's a tough situat . . . HOW THE FUCK DOES SHE NOT KNOW SHE'S FUCKING PREGNANT?! 09:15:25 PM

If anyone thinks I'm sitting through Bachmann, you're out of your goddamn motherfucking minds. 09:22:33 PM

> Michelle Bachmann, Republican congresswoman from Minnesota, gave the "Tea Party" response to Obama's speech.

This "I Didn't Know I Was Pregnant" marathon is on until 2 am. I feel like I've won the motherfucking election already. 09:49:30 PM

A Duck, a Puppy, and a Pillow

Wednesday, January 26, 2011

Oh, hell no, this hotel has a motherfucking breakfast buffet? And it's fucking free? Hell yes I'll have a pancake, thanks. 07:28:10 AM

Sweet fucking Jesus, all the fucking coffee I can drink? Bring it fucking on. 07:30:16 AM

■ ■ ■

I've been shaking hands outside of PetSmart all morning. Last day I let Hambone and Quaxelrod set my fucking schedule. 11:56:16 AM

Now I'm doing a tour of the city's fucking duck ponds and dog parks. Axelrod's fucking mustache did a better scheduling job than this. 03:13:57 PM

■ ■ ■

Back at the hotel for debate prep. Quaxelrod is filling in for Braun, Hambone is covering Chico, and a pillow from the bed is Del Valle. 05:09:13 PM

> The final candidates in the mayoral race were Rahm Emanuel, Gery Chico, Carol Moseley Braun, Miguel Del Valle, and two lesser-known

candidates who didn't often get invited to the high-profile debates Emanuel would attend: Patricia Van Pelt Watkins and William "Dock" Walls.

Topics covered: lack of old guys tossing bread, repressive off-leash laws, and the handsy maid who works weekends. Fuck. 05:16:35 PM

While Pillow Del Valle and I are in agreement that double starch is too much fucking starch, I'm beginning to think that I need my team back. 05:31:49 PM

I keep getting Peter fucking Gabriel's motherfucking "In Your Eyes" stuck in my fucking head and it's driving me goddamn insane. 07:00:19 PM

I may have underestimated Pillow Del Valle. He's definitely got some good points about the fucking hotel tax. 07:05:28 PM

Debate prep wrapped. I sincerely fucking hope that Chico doesn't lick my face tomorrow as much as Hambone did tonight. 07:23:03 PM

Seriously, this fucking song won't get the fuck out of my fucking head. 10:21:02 PM

Street Legal

Thursday, January 27, 2011

Sweet fucking coffee, you sometimes feel like my only motherfucking friend. 07:32:08 AM

Quaxelrod thinks we should do more debate prep, but I think it's because he gets a fucking bread crumb when he gets a right answer. 07:59:06 AM

Quaxelrod needs a swim, Hambone needs a walk, Pillow Del Valle needs a fluff. Didn't I used to have people who took care of this bullshit? 08:23:30 AM

● ● ●

There's that goddamn motherfucking song again. I'm going to stab myself in the fucking ear soon. 10:58:49 AM

Picking out clothes for the debate tonight. I've got fucking duck shit on most of my suits. 12:12:17 PM

I may just go over in this T-shirt and sweats. The shirt has a sweet fucking tiger on it. Hambone thinks it's bad-ass. 12:17:56 PM

This motherfucking snow is going to make me look ridiculous if I go out in my tiger T-shirt. 03:32:14 PM

■ ■ ■

What the fucking fuck do you mean, no waterfowl in the Chicago City Club? Chico probably got his motherfucking guinea hen in! 04:24:06 PM

And I totally see Braun strutting around with her fucking rooster. But no goddamn ducks? For fucking shame, man. For. Fucking. Shame. 04:35:41 PM

Why did it just get so fucking quiet in here? 05:00:15 PM

> The Illinois Supreme Court had just overturned the Appellate Court ruling, stating:
>
>> "So there will be no mistake, let us be entirely clear. This court's decision is based on the following and only on the following: (1) what it means to be a resident for election purposes was clearly established long ago, and Illinois law has been consistent on the matter since at least the 19th century; (2) the novel standard adopted by the Appellate Court majority is without any foundation in Illinois law; (3) the board's factual findings were not against the manifest weight of the evidence; and (4) the board's decision was not clearly erroneous."

MOTHERFUCKING STREET LEGAL, BITCHES! 05:08:20 PM

Hambone is fucking humping every fucking leg in sight. 05:12:05 PM

Huh. Feel a little stupid about the whole fucking apartment trashing thing now. 05:14:49 PM

FUCK THE DEBATE, LET'S HOLD THE MOTHERFUCKING ELECTION RIGHT FUCKING NOW. 05:17:29 PM

Shotgunning motherfucking cans of motherfucking beer two at a goddamn time! 05:24:02 PM

Just ran up to the other sorry fucking candidates and yelled, "MOTHERFUCKING WINNING THE MOTHERFUCKING FUTURE!" 05:36:23 PM

You stupid fucking fucks have to debate me now. BRING IT THE FUCK ON! 05:39:19 PM

> It really was remarkable timing, the announcement coming just two hours before the debate.

God, I fucking wish Axelrod and Carl the Intern were here right now. Who's going to hold my fucking feet for the keg stands? 05:40:59 PM

Axelrod would probably be wearing his beer hat right now, grinning like the motherfucking Cheshire fucking Cat. Fucking where are you? 05:45:54 PM

And Carl. Jesus, seemed like that kid's heart just shattered in two on Monday. He'd probably be up on Axelrod's fucking shoulders right now. 05:51:13 PM

Ah, fuck it. TOSS ME ANOTHER MOTHERFUCKING BEER, WE'RE WINNING THIS MOTHERFUCKING ELECTION! 05:55:30 PM

Holy fucking fuck, that fucking Peter fucking Gabriel song is back in my fucking head. Just what I fucking need. 06:29:50 PM

Reached in my pocket and pulled out Axelrod's Disneyland pen. I gave him my fucking heart. He gave me a MousekePen. 06:46:11 PM

> "I gave her my heart, she gave me a pen": Lloyd Dobler's saddest line in *Say Anything*.

Alright, bitches, let's debate this shit. 06:58:29 PM

I'm stabbing Axelrod's MousekePen into my thigh every time the motherfucking camera cuts away—17 more fucking minutes. 07:43:14 PM

Also, I'm pretty fucking sure Braun is dozing off right now. 07:44:15 PM

Chico thinks he smells fucking amazing, but the rest of us were joking about "eau de Chico" backstage. Right next to him, it's overpowering. 07:46:35 PM

Hambone fucking drilled me on these goddamn facts and figures. I think I fucking nailed them 99% of the time. 07:50:08 PM

I'm about to meet the challenge of changing out of this fucking suit. Almost fucking done. 07:56:54 PM

Goddamn it, there's that fucking song again. Do you fucking hear it? I fucking swear Chico looked up when it started up. 07:57:54 PM

Hambone thinks it went well, but I hate these fucking things. I don't want to sell anything, buy anything, or process anything in a debate. 08:01:04 PM

I don't want to fucking sell anything bought or processed, or buy anything sold or processed, or process anything sold, bought, or processed. 08:02:22 PM

You know, in a motherfucking debate. 08:02:59 PM

> This was all a riff on another line from *Say Anything*: "I don't want to sell anything, buy anything, or process anything as a career. I don't want to sell anything bought or processed, or buy anything sold or processed, or process anything sold, bought, or processed, or repair anything sold, bought, or processed. You know, as a career, I don't want to do that." Fits better here than broken up over Tweets.

Anyway, that shit's over. One more of these motherfucking things. Then I never have to hang out with those three fucking people again. 08:04:47 PM

But seriously, that fucking Peter fucking Gabriel song is getting louder. Hambone says I'm crazy, but it's really goddamn loud now. 08:06:46 PM

■ ■ ■

HOLY FUCKING SHIT! There're Axelrod and Carl the Intern, standing on the roof of the goddamn Civic, boom boxes over their heads. 08:15:24 PM

And a week of references to *Say Anything* culminates in the iconic image from the film: Cusack standing in the rain, boom box over his head, Peter Gabriel's "In Your Eyes" blasting out.

They're blaring that fucking Peter Gabriel song! And they're fucking smiling fucking huge smiles! And it's snowing. And it's beautiful. 08:17:16 PM

And Quaxelrod is fucking flying circles around their heads, and fucking Hambone leapt up onto the roof of the car. And I'm fucking crying. 08:18:26 PM

I'm crying like a baby, because this has been a motherfucking week from fucking hell, and here we all are, on Michigan Avenue, in the snow. 08:20:41 PM

We're all fucking crying and laughing and barking and quacking and the city has never looked more beautiful, and in four weeks I'll be mayor. 08:25:30 PM

It turns out Carl the Intern and Axelrod didn't crash Axelrod's Civic into City Hall. They went down to motherfucking Springfield instead. 08:29:56 PM

Carl just looked at me, and said, "What did you expect? I told you we'd Supreme this shit, so we motherfucking Supremed this shit." 08:31:00 PM

Now we're all crammed into Axelrod's fucking Civic—the ceiling's still dented in—driving down Lake Shore Drive, just fucking freestyling. 08:38:32 PM

"Let's break out of this fake ass Party / and turn this in to a Classic Night / If we die in each other's arms . . ." 08:39:30 PM

Back Together

Friday, January 28, 2011

This Holiday Inn Express breakfast buffet is about to get fucked like it's never been fucked before. 07:33:03 AM

Carl the Intern and Axelrod are in a pancake-eating contest.
Motherfucking artists at work. 08:01:04 AM

■ ■ ■

Cannonballs in the motherfucking pool. Quaxelrod is the judge. I
got a 7.3. 09:16:53 AM

It's Axelrod and this seven-year-old girl named Alyssa in the finals,
both tied at 9.8. The whole cleaning crew is here, fucking cheering.
09:31:06 AM

Holy fucking Jesus fuck, little Alyssa just pulled a triple-flip
cannonball to win this shit. Axelrod's pouting in his Speedo.
09:51:20 AM

■ ■ ■

Out apartment hunting. Again. It's fucking hard to find a place
that'll take both a dog and a duck. 12:23:14 PM

Couldn't find an apartment. Just moving into the crawlspace of my
old house. Nobody tell the fucking asshole upstairs. 04:43:37 PM

Holy fucking fuck, it's finally motherfucking Friday fucking night.
Longest fucking week ever. 05:03:56 PM

No furniture down here yet, so we're just sitting on boxes passing
a bottle. Axelrod found a box of Legos, so he's in fucking heaven.
05:35:57 PM

Best part of being down here is that I get to wear my grandfather's
pleather jacket. I look like motherfucking Fonzie. Aaaaay.
05:41:01 PM

Just opened a box: motherfucking Twister! This night just got in-
fucking-sane! 06:54:28 PM

Saturday, January 29, 2011

Motherfucking Saturday meetings need to be constitutionally
illegal. 09:02:43 AM

I mean fucking seriously, you spend five fucking days a week being fucked in the ass by meetings. We really need to make it six? 09:06:47 AM

Text from Plouffe: "Just lube up your asshole then, because you're recording robocalls today." Fuck. 09:09:35 AM

On take fucking forty-six of these robocalls. I'm this fucking close to biting the fucking head off this fucking microphone. 10:13:03 AM

Motherfucking take fucking one hundred and twenty fucking six. 10:30:21 AM

Fucking nailed it on take four fifty three. Ring ring, motherfuckers, I'm calling you up. 12:22:43 PM

■ ■ ■

Just found a box of sheets in the crawlspace. We're going to cut out eyeholes and haunt the fuck out of Halpin upstairs. 06:27:19 PM

BOO! You stupid motherfucker. 07:01:41 PM

Hambone looks fucking spooky as shit in his ghost sheet. 07:16:34 PM

Carl the Intern is wearing my wife's wedding dress under his sheet. "I'm the fucking 'Ghost Bride.'" 07:36:09 PM

Sunday, January 30, 2011

Axelrod has built a scale model of all of fucking Egypt out of Legos. It looks fucking amazing. 10:06:22 AM

> The uprising in Egypt that began on January 25 and would end on February 11, with Mubarak stepping down, had become a major demonstration of Twitter's power to disseminate information in real-time from far-flung regions of the world.

A whole crowd of Barbies just set the Ministry of Information on fucking Lego fire. 10:33:08 AM

A Barrel O Monkeys is trying to loot the Lego museum, but they're being stopped by a floppy sheriff doll and a spaceman toy. 10:41:24 AM

There's a toy standoff in front of the Lincoln Logs Department of the Interior. The My Pretty Ponies refuse to move the fuck along. 11:05:21 AM

Oh fuck. Quaxelrod just ate Lego Mubarak. 11:29:47 AM

Cheer up, Tweedy

Spent all goddamn day at the vet getting that goddamn Lego out of Quaxelrod. Now running late to Tweedy's fucking fund-raiser. 05:47:11 PM

> Jeff Tweedy headlined a fund-raiser for Emanuel at the Park West Theater in Chicago.

Tweedy's being pissy because he doesn't want to play any Black Eyed Peas songs. What the fuck? People love that shit. 07:18:52 PM

Not saying they're a good band—they're fucking terrible—but if you want people with money to give that shit away, play the Black Eyed Peas. 07:21:54 PM

But no, Tweedy's pulling this fucking "I'm in Wilco, so I'm going to play Wilco songs" bullshit, like he knows anything about fund-raising. 07:23:07 PM

I told him that he can stuff his fucking guitar up his ass and go play for Chico—he'll make his troubadour ass play Bieber. 07:25:05 PM

So it goes without fucking saying that he's going out there and playing "I Gotta Feeling" right fucking now. 07:26:44 PM

Also, would it fucking kill this motherfucker to smile every now and then? Cheer up, Tweedy! 07:42:26 PM

Monday, January 31, 2011

Jesus fucking Christ, I just woke up in the back of the Wilco van. My bongo hand feels like it's fucking broken. 08:40:11 AM

Storm Warnings

Got back to the crawlspace and Axelrod's stockpiling canned goods. He just keeps muttering "storm coming." Fuck this shit. 09:41:19 AM

> The National Weather Service issued an alert that 20-plus inches of snow was expected to hit Chicago on Tuesday. News reports at the time said that this could be the third largest snow to hit the Chicago area. On top of the snow were reports warning of extremely high winds—gusts up to 50 mph, creating 15- to 20-foot waves crashing onto Lake Shore Drive. To put it another way, as the *Chicago Tribune*'s Weather Center blog did: "Winds and snow likely to combine to make a monster."

Axelrod handed me a shopping list and said, "We don't have much time." The fuck do we need oxygen tanks for? 10:02:08 AM

Also on Axelrod's Storm Survival list: 100 copies of today's Chicago fucking Tribune and 100 newspaper-sized picture frames. 10:13:02 AM

I asked Axelrod about the fucking newspapers. "It's for preservation for future generations, in case we don't survive the storm . . ." 10:21:38 AM

". . . the fact that I'm on the cover is just pure fucking coincidence." But he's fucking smiling. 10:22:30 AM

> The real David Axelrod's face was the entire cover of the newsstand edition of the *Chicago Tribune* as he announced he was moving back to Chicago from Washington to head up President Obama's 2012 re-election bid.

Axelrod has Carl the Intern smoking meats down here. This whole crawlspace smells fucking incredible. 10:50:54 AM

Axelrod's list calls for 20 shovels, but I've hit 6 stores and only have 18. Fuck. 02:01:39 PM

Axelrod's response? "You want to be the asshole out there shoveling with his hands when we break the 18th shovel, just stop looking." 02:02:20 PM

■ ■ ■

The motherfucking health-care law is ruled un-fucking-constitutional? Fuck this motherfucking bullshit. 02:14:44 PM

A federal judge in Florida struck down the entire health-care law, ruling that the mandate that everyone have insurance is unconstitutional. The issue, of course, is continuing to work its way through the courts.

Fuck Florida, fuck district courts, and fuck those tea-shitting fuck-party assholes. I worked too fucking hard on that bill. 02:29:34 PM

Is it a pre-existing condition when every fucking health-care opponent is a fucking cancer in my ass? 02:36:03 PM

Carl the Intern just asked if I need him to go Supreme this health-care bullshit too. The kid learns fucking fast. 02:45:00 PM

■ ■ ■

Snow preparations finally done. Axelrod just passed out our motherfucking sleeping shifts. "Everyone gets two hours on watch. *Everyone.*" 05:19:15 PM

The snowsuits Axelrod made for Hambone and Quaxelrod are adorable. Tiny fucking snowshoes. Tiny fucking hats. 05:20:53 PM

Finished my first two-hour snow-watch shift. So far, it's just really fucking cold. Hambone's up next. 09:52:33 PM

Motherfucking Thundersnow

Tuesday, February 1, 2011

Sweet fucking coffee. Axelrod had us buy 20 pounds of beans to weather the storm. I fucking doubled that. 07:15:37 AM

Axelrod's built a cubicle out of oversized pork 'n' beans cans. He calls it "the weathercenter." It's been beeping all fucking night.
07:24:30 AM

Report from Axelrod's weathercenter has the big storm hitting later this afternoon. Perfectly fucking reasonable to get drunk now. 07:40:06

Irish motherfucking coffee for the fucking win. 07:41:38 AM

■ ■ ■

Public service announcement: in about three hours, you're going to need a lot of fucking whiskey. 12:49:49 PM

The storm was predicted to hit at about 3:00 in the afternoon.

Axelrod's outside just bellowing, "THE WIND IS PICKING THE MOTHERFUCK UP!" 12:54:58 PM

Axelrod's outside screaming, "IT'S FUCKING HERE! IT'S FUCKING HERE!" 03:25:55 PM

Axelrod's got a line of Teamster trucks parked outside and he's attaching plows to them. Motherfucking shovel fucking ready. 03:53:08 PM

That's right, Chico, Braun, and Del Valle, what do you got? Don't bring a motherfucking shovel to a plow fight. 03:56:54 PM

Oh fuck. I already ate all the motherfucking Oreos. Thinking about sending Carl the Intern out to pick up more. 04:05:49 PM

Axelrod just came in for a quick check-in at the weathercenter. His eyes are shining like motherfucking beacons. "This is my time." 04:09:38 PM

Sending Carl the Intern out on a sled, with Quaxelrod and Hambone mushing. Hope he's back with the fucking Oreos soon. 04:16:53 PM

Looking out the periscope Axelrod hooked up. I'm pretty fucking sure snow isn't supposed to fall UP. What the fucking fuck. 04:33:21 PM

Plan: When this shit is over, massive fucking snowball fight on Ravenswood. East side of tracks vs. west side. 04:44:04 PM

A giant fucking snowball rolled against the crawlspace door. It busted open and out fell Carl the Intern, Hambone, Quaxelrod, and my Oreos. 05:20:09 PM

■ ■ ■

Axelrod just called in from a Teamster truck. "We're going to go surf a plow on the lake. You in?" Fuck yes I'm in. 07:26:40 PM

The plan: we're going to hit velocity on the Michigan Ave curve, launch into the water, and ride a motherfucking 18' wave to victory. 07:31:45 PM

Holy fuck. Unless you've got a fleet of Teamsters to drive you around, STAY THE FUCK INSIDE. It's insane out here. 07:41:33 PM

Me, I've got a fleet of Teamsters, and we're barreling down Milwaukee. ACES FUCKING HIGH, YOU MOTHERFUCKING STORM. 07:45:45 PM

Up on the roof of the cab, heading north down Lake Shore fast. Curve's coming up. Time to hang the fuck on . . . 07:56:45 PM

. . . and we're off the curve and in the goddamn air, flying. The wind and water are like wild animals fucking. 08:02:28 PM

We caught the wave! It's a fucking 20-fucking footer, all fucking gray and ice and snarl. 08:04:33 PM

Balanced on the roof of this plow cab, riding a fucking ice wave, in the middle of the worst fucking blizzard in a generation. 08:06:30 PM

I'M THE FUCKING KING OF THE MOTHERFUCKING WORLD! 08:06:41 PM

> Lake Shore Drive was a disaster zone that night. The storm hit just before the evening commute and the roadway became dangerous. Three accidents between 7:15 and 7:45 pm slowed traffic down, and, as the snow, ice, and winds enveloped vehicles, they became stuck. Some drivers were in their cars for more than 12 hours. Others abandoned their cars on the roadway. In all, the city had to tow more than 500 abandoned cars off Lake Shore Drive.

■ ■ ■

Back at the crawlspace, hot toddies all the fuck around. Fucking stay the fuck warm, bitches. 08:45:22 PM

...

MOTHERFUCKING THUNDERFUCKINGSNOW ALL UP IN HERE.
10:22:52 PM

> Seriously, *thundersnow*. For real. I'd seen a fair number of blizzards in Chicago, but I'd never seen anything like that.

Dig Me Out

Wednesday, February 2, 2011

HOLY FUCK. IT IS INFUCKINGSANE OUTSIDE. 08:47:41 AM

> The official snowfall total for the blizzard was 20.2 inches. But because of the high winds and the fine-grained quality of the snow, there was a ton of drifting, leaving some spots almost snowless and others buried under many feet of snow.

A downside to living in the crawlspace under my rented house: We're fucking snowed the fuck in. Not in—snowed fucking under.
08:58:45 AM

Carl the Intern is designing a tunnel to get us the fuck out. "The key is that it doesn't collapse in on itself while we're inside." 09:01:15 AM

Carl the Intern has emptied all the pork 'n' beans onto the crawlspace floor and is welding the cans together into a fucking escape elevator. 10:40:52 AM

When he presented the plans to me and Axelrod, he said, "It's pretty simple, really: we're going to Chilean Miner this shit."
10:42:28 AM

I get the pork 'n' beans elevator, but I'm still a little unclear on how we're actually digging the motherfucking escape tunnel.
10:45:26 AM

Carl's got Hambone tunneling five shafts out, which will result in a "controlled implosion." Yeah, that sounds fucking safe. 10:59:26 AM

Where did Carl learn all this? "I'm in the Junior Engineering Club at Lane Tech." Fuck yes. Hambone, get those paws digging! 11:02:11 AM

Lane Tech is one of the top high schools in the city. A selective-enrollment school of 4,200 students, it boasts that it has produced more students who have gone on to earn PhDs than any other high school in the country.

Hambone's done digging the shafts, now Carl'll trigger the implosion and we ride this pork elevator to fucking freedom. 11:20:26 AM

■ ■ ■

And we're out. Holy fuck, it's fucking Hoth out here. Axelrod's handing out the goddamn shovels. Let's get digging. 11:37:08 AM

What's up, motherfucking sun—nice to see you. A little fucking late, though. 11:55:09 AM

Sun's out, streets are mostly clear. MOTHERFUCKING SNOWBALL FUCKING FIGHT. 02:49:13 PM

■ ■ ■

Jesus fucking Christ, my arms fucking ache from all that fucking shoveling. Quaxelrod can barely lift his little wings. 05:05:29 PM

Carl the Intern built an igloo, and we're all just lying around in here, fucking whiskied and exhausted. Stay fucking warm. 06:27:55 PM

Arctic Exploration

Thursday, February 3, 2011

Motherfucking sweet fucking coffee. We're drinking it in motherfucking snow cups. 07:47:16 AM

Strategy session in the igloo: Plouffe's in over speakerphone. We can't understand a single motherfucking word he's saying. 08:10:59 AM

Seriously, this is fucking Plouffe: "I . . . hrm . . . kit . . . fuck . . . and . . . shit . . . Quaxelrod . . . log." How the fuck does this fucking help? 08:20:41 AM

Fuck it, we've all left the igloo, just playing with Hambone in the snow. Plouffe's still on speaker being unin-fucking-telligible. 08:25:45 AM

We're all in our fucking Arctic-grade snowsuits, just wandering. Axelrod's eyes are lit up. "It's like we're the last people on Earth." 09:33:30 AM

> Following the massive snowstorm, the temperature dropped into the single digits.

It really does feel like the end of the fucking world. We're walking down the middle of the motherfucking Dan Ryan right now. 10:09:05 AM

Quaxelrod fucking owns the motherfucking express lanes. Waddling like a bad-ass motherfucker. 10:12:00 AM

The Loop is fucking abandoned. We're swinging from the L tracks like they're motherfucking monkey bars. 10:40:42 AM

Now we're walking out on the lake. It's just one giant fucking sheet of gray fucking ice. And it's just the five of us. 11:22:16 AM

There are a lot of things I can say I've done with my life. But now I can say I made a motherfucking snow angel on Lake Michigan. 12:50:10 PM

Finally ran into another person. And it's someone driving a motherfucking cupcake truck. Fucking cupcakes. 02:05:10 PM

Made it back to the igloo. Ran into a total of four people: cupcake driver, a guy on a donut run, and two canvassers for motherfucking Chico. 03:16:30 PM

■ ■ ■

Carl the Intern did an incredible job on this igloo. It's got a couple of little snow desks, a fridge, some fucking ice couches. 05:44:48 PM

He built a little fireplace, so we're warm in here. And we can actually stand up—major fucking benefit over the crawlspace. 05:46:28 PM

Carl even built a little second floor—sorry, "a lofted atrium"—where Hambone and Quaxelrod can hang out. This place is fucking awesome. 05:54:41 PM

Sitting in the igloo, passing a bottle around. Axelrod busted out his guitar and is singing Bon fucking Jovi. "On a steel horse I ride . . ." 09:07:34 PM

A belly warm with whiskey, a duck and a dog sleeping soundly, and your best friend playing Jovi. Motherfucking awesome. 09:29:40 PM

Friday, February 4, 2011

Motherfucking Jesus fucking Christ, coffee sure tastes absolutely fucking incredible this morning. 07:43:29 AM

Finally digging out Axelrod's Civic. Starting to regret not getting the fucking passenger-side window replaced. 09:18:26 AM

With all this fucking snow, what are the chances of a giant fucking line at Hot Doug's today? Nobody tell Quaxelrod about the duck fat fries. 09:48:07 AM

> Hot Doug's, the "encased meat emporium," is an incredibly popular hot dog and sausage restaurant in Chicago. Lines—especially on Fridays and Saturdays, when owner Doug Sohn offers French fries deep-fried in duck fat—can snake down the block. It is absolutely worth the wait.

■ ■ ■

Motherfucking meetings all afternoon. Don't people understand that it's fucking Friday? 03:43:08 PM

Chicago fucking Tribune endorsement, bitches! Think of how fucking awesome that would be if anyone fucking read a newspaper. 04:38:55 PM

The *Chicago Tribune* released its endorsement of Rahm Emanuel. Couched in warnings of the dire financial straits the city and region are in, the endorsement concluded with the line, "This guy deserves a chance to get this near-impossible job done."

More motherfucking meetings. It's cute that someone still thinks there's a race, but it's cutting into my motherfucking Friday. 05:10:19 PM

Just walked the fuck out of that meeting. Fuck everything: it's Friday fucking night! 06:09:21 PM

The motherfucking party is in the motherfucking igloo tonight. 07:05:23 PM

Early and Often

Saturday, February 5, 2011

Coffee, bitches. The secret is motherfucking coffee. 08:10:52 AM

Visiting early voting centers today. If you want to stop by, I'll be the fucking guy wearing the giant foam voting booth. 08:30:20 AM

■ ■ ■

Chico just showed up wearing a huge inflatable Chico costume, and he's pretending to use my foam booth to vote. Fuck. 10:11:00 AM

Great, now Braun's here—regular size—and she's fucking pretending to vote too. Why the fuck aren't there armholes in this fucking suit? 10:39:30 AM

Del Valle just arrived and is taking inflatable Chico to task for double-fucking voting. Ha fucking ha. 11:09:49 AM

He started out saying, "This giant foam voting booth is sacred."
Then I tuned him out just like every fucking other time Del Valle
talks. 11:15:11 AM

■ ■ ■

Holy fuck, foam-rubber costumes really stiffen up when you're out
in the fucking cold all day. 04:48:25 PM

Shuffling my way back to the igloo now, this frozen foam voting
booth is like walking around in a fucking block of wood. 04:54:21 PM

■ ■ ■

Carl the Intern just finished splicing into the asshole's cable, so
now this motherfucking igloo gets 148 channels. HGTV, bitches.
07:52:01 PM

House Hunters is on next. Axelrod is motherfucking beside himself.
"Which goddamn house are they going to choose?" 09:49:05 PM

House number one? What the fuck is that bullshit?! I'd give the rest
of my fucking fingerstub for house number three! 10:25:34 PM

> The fingerstub should probably be addressed. Rahm is missing most
> of his middle finger on his right hand. President Obama himself has
> made the joke you just did, saying at a 2005 roast of Emanuel that
> the accident "rendered him practically mute." The accident itself
> happened in high school, while he was operating a meat slicer at the
> Arby's where he worked. In a 2010 interview with a visibly queasy
> Katie Couric (which he opened by warning "I hope nobody had lunch
> here"), he explained that he sliced the finger "deep into the bone; it
> was hanging by a thread." Instead of going to a hospital, he wrapped
> the finger himself, accidentally trapping some meat inside. He ended
> up "with five blood infections, two bone infections, gangrene, seven
> weeks in the hospital, a 105 fever, and [being] about one day away
> from looking at the other side of the ledger." So yeah, that's *super* gross.

I'm living in a motherfucking igloo, and you assholes choose a
piece of shit house like number one? Fuck these fucking House
Hunters. 10:33:53 PM

Snowmad

Sunday, February 6, 2011

Oh great, just what we need: more motherfucking, goddamn, shit-assing snow. 07:36:18 AM

Axelrod is insisting that he has this fucking shit under control, but we're all a little afraid that he's gone a bit snowmad. 08:24:22 AM

Axelrod's eyes are fucking wild, like Shackleton's on his last expedition. 08:25:47 AM

Axelrod's gripping that shovel a little too tightly, and ranting about crystalline formations. This might not fucking end well. 08:42:50 AM

Pretty sure Axelrod thinks we're all snowmen. He keeps yelling, "Where's your magic fucking top hat, you snowy fucks?"
08:48:47 AM

Holy fuck: He's taking fucking swings at us with his shovel now. We're ducking 'em, but he's taking chunks out of the igloo.
08:58:47 AM

Axelrod's yelling "CORN COB PIPE"—swing—"BUTTON NOSE"—swing—"TWO EYES MADE OUT OF COAL"—swing. We are so fucked. 09:03:36 AM

Carl the Intern, Hambone, and I are backed into a fucking corner here. This may be it for us. Axelrod's got the shovel up over his head. 09:15:41 AM

Jesus fucking Christ, we're all fucking crying here. He's just standing there, quivering, ready to strike. Someone tell Amy I loved her. 09:20:31 AM

> This was the only direct reference to Amy Rule, Rahm Emanuel's wife. She actually stayed in DC during the duration of the mayoral campaign—Emanuel's two children were already enrolled in school there. I doubt this story would have been written had his family moved back too.

HOLY SHIT! IT'S QUAXELROD!! That little fucking duck just swooped in and has Axelrod by the 'stache. We're saved! 09:25:34 AM

It's over. We're all sitting in the igloo together, sobbing. It's been a hard race. Someone was going to fucking snap eventually. 09:43:58 AM

Man, Quaxelrod really took a good chunk off Axelrod's mustache. What a great fucking duck. 09:45:50 AM

Super Bowl XX

Things are good here now. We're all going to head out to brunch and then get busy not watching the motherfucking Super Bowl. 10:00:51 AM

■ ■ ■

Picked up a bucket of chicken, and am settling into the igloo to watch a tape of the 1985 Super Bowl. Go fucking Bears! 05:45:21 PM

The 1985 Super Bowl is legend in Chicago. The Bears vs. the New England Patriots. It was more than a game. The 1985 Chicago Bears were one of the most unforgettable collection of characters ever to assemble on a sports team. Ditka, The Fridge, Jim McMahon, Walter Payton, Samurai Mike Singletary, Steve "Mongo" McMichael, "Speedy" Willie Gault . . . the list could go on. The entire team recorded a song, "The Super Bowl Shuffle," as they progressed through their season; the song featured raps by many of the players.

Ran into Chico while picking up chicken. He said he was watching "just for the commercials," which confirmed that he's a raging douche. 05:54:05 PM

God, I fucking miss you, Sweetness. When you ran the ball, it really was like you were making romance. 05:55:26 PM

"Sweetness" was the nickname of Walter Payton, the storied Bears running back, Hall-of-Famer, and all-around legend. He died in 1999 of complications related to a rare liver disease and cancer. Payton's verse from the Super Bowl Shuffle begins, "Well, they call me Sweetness / And I like to dance. Runnin' the ball is like makin' romance."

Second fucking half of Super Bowl XX. I know how it ends, but I fucking cry every time. Tears of fucking joy. Go Bears. 07:36:23 PM

Christ, we're just watching, rewinding, and rewatching when the Fridge runs in for the motherfucking TD. Go Bears. 08:33:46 PM

The Fridge was a 382-pound defensive lineman for the Bears whose gap-toothed smile and friendly personality made him an overnight star. They even made a G.I. Joe figure based on him. Unfortunately, after I sent out this Tweet, someone @replied with a recent story in *Sports Illustrated* about The Fridge's long battle with alcoholism, his weight, and his overall health. But that moment in Super Bowl XX, when he's brought in and scores a touchdown, really is a memory that most Chicagoans over a certain age have forever burned into their brains (for positive and negative reasons—many Chicagoans are still angry that the play robbed Walter Payton of his only chance to score in the Super Bowl).

God, XX really was the greatest game that was ever fucking played. Our matching '85 Bears sweaters are aglow. 08:42:58 PM

CUE THE SUPER BOWL MOTHERFUCKING SHUFFLE. 08:56:29 PM

Monday, February 7, 2011

Ended up staying up all night rewatching Super Bowl XX over and over. My entire fucking day is going to be fueled by coffee. 07:46:43 AM

Be Like the Unicorn on My T-shirt

Sweet motherfucking coffee, I love you more than I love myself. 07:59:33 AM

■ ■ ■

Working on my economic innovation plan, but really need a motherfucking mustard-out-of-my-shirt plan instead. 12:18:42 PM

You know what doesn't work? Bleach. Now I have a white spot on
my blue shirt, and a motherfucking chemical burn on my chest.
12:34:33 PM

Bleach-burn remedy: lie down shirtless in the snow. It stings for a
minute, but then you don't feel a fucking thing. 01:16:08 PM

■ ■ ■

Best thing about being endorsed by Jesse White is getting to
hang out with the fucking Tumblers. Motherfucking back flips!
04:05:12 PM

> Jesse White has been the secretary of state of Illinois since 1998 and a
> politician in both local and state politics since the '70s. He's perhaps
> better known as the founder and coach of the Jesse White Tumblers,
> a "juvenile delinquency prevention program" active since 1959 that
> teaches kids responsibility through tumbling exhibitions. More than
> 13,000 kids have been involved in the program since its inception;
> they've toured around the world, performed for presidents, been on
> *Letterman* ("as well as several performances on Nippon Television in
> Tokyo"), and are generally amazing.

HOLY FUCK: Carl the Intern can fucking flip clear over the
goddamn igloo. The Jesse White Tumblers are going fucking nuts!
04:46:12 PM

Axelrod just tried to clear the igloo too, and now we've got an
Axelrod-shaped hole in the wall. Fuck. 04:52:23 PM

Also, he appears to have a pretty fucking wicked concussion. Just
fucking perfect. 04:56:36 PM

■ ■ ■

Do yourself a favor, and don't look at the motherfucking weather
report for the next few days. 09:17:03 PM

> Single digit temperatures—dipping below zero most overnights—
> dominated the five-day forecast.

We've sent Carl the Intern out to harpoon a motherfucking whale
so we can use the blubber to keep warm. 09:24:22 PM

Tuesday, February 8, 2011

Been carving whale blubber since Carl got back. Upsides: so motherfucking warm. Downsides: it really fucks up a suit. 07:44:07 AM

Now that these fucking blubber coats are finished, Axelrod wants to go hunt saber-toothed cats, but I was thinking mastodon ride. 07:49:31 AM

Before you give me shit about my whale blubber coat, I'm pretty sure I saw a Groupon ad that said it was OK. 07:54:11 AM

> Groupon debuted its first TV ads during the Super Bowl, and the media coverage over the next couple of days was intense. Conceived as tongue-in-cheek parodies of celebrity endorsements of causes, Groupon's ad included saving the whales and the rain forest. But it was one about the plight of the Tibetan people that raised the most ire. "The people of Tibet are in trouble," the ad, narrated by actor Timothy Hutton, explained. "Their very culture [is] in jeopardy . . . but they still whip up an amazing fish curry. And since 200 of us bought on Groupon.com, we're getting $30 worth of Tibetan food for just $15." It's probably no surprise that the joke-URL the ads pointed to, savethemoney.org, is no longer active.

Riding a mastodon over to unveil my economic innovation plan. It's so fucking cold even the mastodon is shivering. 09:17:21 AM

■ ■ ■

Unveiling my economic innovation plan at a novelty T-shirt company. Yes, the irony is so motherfucking palpable you could put it on a shirt. 09:34:55 AM

> It was back to Threadless for Rahm Emanuel to talk budget and the economy. He announced a $75 million spending freeze, and a plan to build a "Google-like" tech campus in Chicago, among other proposals.

Axelrod fucking loves this place: "I'm voting up 715 different designs with mustaches on them." 09:42:42 AM

Original plan was to do this speech at Groupon, but now everyone thinks they're fucking assholes. Note to self: lay off the Tibet jokes. 09:50:21 AM

So now I'm talking about innovation in a warehouse, wearing a T-shirt with a unicorn on it. Actually, that part's fucking awesome.
09:55:34 AM

This is the second time I've been to this place, and they still insist on giving me a tour. It's still just giant fucking boxes of shirts.
10:02:43 AM

Speech preview: "We're Chicago. Maybe—just fucking maybe—we can build something better than stupid T-shirts and half-off deals."
10:08:22 AM

Speech preview: "I remember when Daniel Burnham kicked the fucking world in the nuts. Let's get back to being a town of fucking nut-kickers." 10:11:36 AM

Speech preview: "Because somehow this town has confused driving fucking cupcakes around with goddamn innovation."
10:14:54 AM

Speech preview: "So, Chicago, let's stop screwing around. Let's be like the unicorn on my T-shirt: fucking incredible." 10:18:20 AM

Speech preview: "You can fuck around with stupid shit all you want, but in the meantime New York is making us look like chumps. Again." 10:29:31 AM

And then the plan is to just lead everyone in chanting "FUCK NEW YORK!" and fucking high-five the shit out of everyone. 10:30:29 AM

Icy Salvation

Burning whale blubber in the igloo tonight. It's motherfucking warm, but it smells like death. 07:22:53 PM

Axelrod keeps checking the thermometer and announcing the temperature as it plunges. It's like we're descending into a frozen fucking hell. 08:49:55 PM

"Five degrees." This whale blubber had better be all they say it is, or we're going to be frozen fucking fish sticks by morning. 09:12:41 PM

Wednesday, February 9, 2011

Sweet fucking Jesus, thank you for these motherfucking coffee-sicles. They bring icy salvation. 07:24:16 AM

Hambone just delivered new poll numbers. Fifty-four percent? I think I can feel my motherfucking toes again. 07:34:06 AM

> ABC 7 released a poll that had Rahm Emanuel 40 points above his closest competitor, Gery Chico, who had 14%.

We've carved out a sledding hill in the shape of Braun's poll trends, but we're all scared to try it: too fucking steep. 07:46:19 AM

> Carol Moseley Braun, who had enjoyed a bump to 26% in early January following the dual dropouts of Davis and Meeks, had dropped precipitously in polling, to fourth place, with just 6%.

Axelrod tried it, and I think he woke up half of Ravenswood screaming as he went down, "Ride of a fucking lifetime!" 07:55:19 AM

Danny Davis just showed up with a sled and a hair dryer. "I'm going to sled your damn Mt. Braun and then melt it into motherfucking nothing." 08:11:25 AM

■ ■ ■

When this fucking race is over, I swear to fucking god, I'm going on a motherfucking vacation somewhere warm. 02:10:16 PM

Whoever thought it was a good idea to hold a fucking election in February is getting a motherfucking cock punch on the 23rd. 02:41:29 PM

Plouffe just e-mailed video of a new ad. I think it's fucking adorable that he still thinks there's a race going on. 04:35:32 PM

■ ■ ■

CODE FUCKING RED: whoever scheduled me to be at both a candidate forum and a debate tonight is going on my cock-punch list. 06:13:40 PM

The blizzard the previous week had forced the *Chicago Defender*—the long-running newspaper for the African-American community—to reschedule its mayoral debate. As it turned out, they moved it to the same night that a gay and lesbian organization, LGBT Change, had scheduled a candidate forum. That meant that candidates—who had committed to both, and who didn't want to give up a chance to talk with these constituencies—had to race across town from one to the other. The *Defender* debate was the first to include all six candidates on the ballot (most snubbed Watkins and Walls).

The only thing getting me through this bullfuck of a night is visualizing that I'm somewhere else. Somewhere warm. With a water slide. 06:34:11 PM

■ ■ ■

Forum and debate complete. Now it's time to lock myself in a bathroom and scream for about ninety motherfucking minutes. 08:13:11 PM

The debate was a pile-on on Emanuel, with Watkins whipping the crowd into a frenzy at times. As the *Chicago Sun-Times* reported, "Watkins often stood up to make her points, telling the crowd they had not seen much of her because the media had ignored her. That only made the cheers louder."

Nope, screaming didn't help one fucking bit. Going to end up washing that debate down with a pint of motherfucking whiskey. 09:51:41 PM

Madness? This is Google!

Thursday, February 10, 2011

Hanging out with nerds at Google today. Up half the night building up my elfin sorcerer, in case anyone throws down a motherfucking 20-side. 07:27:46 AM

The Google Chicago office hosted a Fireside chat with Emanuel as part of its "Candidates@Google" series. It was the first candidate event outside of Google's Mountain View campus. In the introduction to the talk, David Lieber jokingly said, "If you look around, you'll notice that there are no media present here today. We did, however, extend an invite to @MayorEmanuel to live-tweet the event. Unfortunately, he's holed up in an igloo with Carl the Intern." They didn't actually extend that invite.

That said, I may need a chalice of motherfucking mead to help me deal with these geeks. 07:29:58 AM

Carl the Intern is beside himself with excitement though. He's been reciting the digits in motherfucking pi for an hour now. 07:33:51 AM

3.14159265 . . . great, now this bullshit is stuck in my motherfucking head too. 07:39:13 AM

Axelrod's having me memorize Monty Python lines—"You know, for the nerds"—but I think he just wants someone to fucking do them with him. 07:47:08 AM

If I understood half of what was in this speech, I'd feel a lot less nervous. What the fucking fuck is a "persistent data store"? 07:52:06 AM

Carl just spent 15 minutes trying to explain what a "multiverse" is. You mean there're other me's? My head fucking hurts. 08:10:00 AM

I need a break from all this hobbiton, time-travel, multiverse bullshit. Where's my fucking New York Times? 08:23:06 AM

The New York Times that morning had run the story "Fake Twitter Accounts Get Real Laughs," which opened with @MayorEmanuel's snow-bound adventures from the previous week. This was also where the idea of a multiverse was introduced.

Axelrod just came out in his "Tron" outfit and Carl is changing into his wizarding cloak. I just look like a fucking chump in a suit. 08:45:40 AM

Well this is the first talk I've ever given where half of the audience is on motherfucking Segways. 10:21:45 AM

Eric Schmidt just wheeled in on his Segway, and is circling me, tossing fucking headfakes. 10:25:41 AM

Former Google CEO Eric Schmidt wasn't actually at the Chicago event. It was hosted by Jim Lecinski, head of the Chicago office.

I might have to do a motherfucking Bing search to figure out a way out of here. 10:27:56 AM

Schmidt wheels right up to my fucking face and says, "I know what you're thinking: maybe I should have taken the blue pill." 10:30:27 AM

Another alternate-dimension reference, this time from *The Matrix*.

Don't ask me how it happened, but we're out on Kinzie right now getting ready to Segway joust. I'm so fucking fucked. 12:06:57 PM

A quick note about Segways: The whole Segway section was an homage to Brian "Fitz" Fitzpatrick, the head of engineering of the Chicago office, a friend who actually owns and uses a Segway. I wrote this entire section mainly to freak him out, but it turns out he was on a cruise in New Zealand at the time.

Holy fuck. You don't quite understand pain until you've been knocked on your ass by a nerd on a Segway. 12:14:13 PM

Schmidt's just wheeling back and forth, yelling, "YOU WANT SOME MORE, BITCH?" I assure you that I didn't even want it the first fucking time. 12:19:02 PM

Now Schmidt's giving a speech that Axelrod says is from the movie "300," but I wouldn't know, 'cause I'm not a fucking nerd. 12:22:29 PM

I have no idea what he's even saying, but Axelrod tells me when Schmidt gets to the line, "Madness? THIS IS GOOGLE!" we need to fucking run. 12:26:56 PM

Running. Holy fuck, we're running. And we're being pursued by 300 fucking geeks. Geeks with motherfucking swords. 12:33:59 PM

Hiding out under the LaSalle bridge. We can hear the fucking Google Segways overhead, but figure they'll run out of batteries eventually. 12:46:39 PM

You know, shit like this never happened back when I was a fucking dancer. 12:56:07 PM

• • •

Made it back to the igloo. Eric Schmidt and his fucking Google Goons finally wheeled away when they realized they were missing "Stargate SG1." 07:50:11 PM

Winding Down the Campaign Trail

You know what this day needs? A motherfucking debate. Here we go. 09:30:51 PM

It was the Fox affiliates' turn to host a mayoral debate. This one, again, with all six candidates.

I swear to fucking god, there are more people asking questions than answering them in this debate. 09:34:58 PM

The debate, which was moderated by Fox anchors Bob Sirott and Robin Robinson, also featured three additional reporters from other Chicago media asking questions and a crawl along the bottom of viewer-submitted observations. It was a very confusing debate to watch.

Wait a second: What the fuck is a nanotechnology again? Just really small shit? 09:44:04 PM

And also: WHAT THE FUCK WAS THAT ALL ABOUT? 09:44:26 PM

Holy fuck, we're saved: invest in nanotech and hardware stores. Can I just walk out? Is that allowed? 09:48:41 PM

William "Dock" Walls included an investment in nanotechnology as one of his tentpole economic policy issues. He was, in fact, the only candidate in the race to have an entire section of his website dedicated to nanotechnology, the practice of building with atomic and molecular-level particles.

We can answer questions just based on reviews we've read about shit? That's awesome, because I have Yelp fucking ready to go. LET'S DO THIS. 09:54:09 PM

> One of the questions asked in the debate was whether any candidate had seen the David Guggenheim–directed documentary *Waiting for Superman,* about inequities in the public school system: Braun raised her hand, but then admitted that she'd not seen the film, but had watched the trailer and seen reviews.

Where have I been scared in this city? HOLY FUCK THIS IS THE DUMBEST FUCKING DEBATE EVER. 10:10:47 PM

> An actual question in the debate: Emanuel and Chico were asked where they had been scared for their own safety in Chicago. Really.

You know what? Quaxelrod was right: everyone in this race is motherfucking crazy. 10:12:52 PM

End of a stupid fucking debate means it's time to get stupid fucking drunk. 10:36:59 PM

Friday, February 11, 2011

Dear coffee, you are the motherfucking greatest of all of mankind's inventions. 07:25:58 AM

So now we have to endure Chico strutting around like a motherfucking peacock because he's only losing by 30 points, huh? 07:39:32 AM

> A new ABC 7 poll showed Emanuel dropping below 50% to 49% and Chico moving up to 19%.

Axelrod's doing TV this morning, which is a bummer because he was going to help fortify the igloo for the coming melt. Fuck. 07:43:40 AM

Hambone brought in today's itinerary: some motherfucking map company. Great. More fucking nerds. 09:37:18 AM

For all the nerds I've put up with this week, I'd better spend every fucking day next week being dunked by Derrick Rose. 09:38:50 AM

I'd had an idea early on that Mayor Daley would admit to @MayorEmanuel that he let Michael Jordan dunk him during the Bulls' NBA dominance of the 1990s. Ended up giving the image to Derrick Rose instead.

I have completely run out of shit to say to nerds. Maybe I'll just give them a word problem and be done with this fucking bullshit. 10:15:15 AM

If someone could actually tell me what this motherfucking company actually does, that'd be a big fucking help. Everywhat? 10:26:37 AM

Another situation, similar to Google, when Rahm Emanuel visited a company where friends of mine work. This time it was the geolocational information company Everyblock.

Carl the Intern is trying to explain it to me, but if he says "geo"-anything one more fucking time, I'm walking out. 10:28:12 AM

I'm geolocating my ass out of this fucking place. Here's to a motherfucking geek-free weekend. 11:34:47 AM

■ ■ ■

Oh my fucking god, it is not goddamn snowing again, is it? 01:44:59 PM

Carl the Intern is sketching out designs for an airplane that we can fly up into these fucking snow clouds. It's motherfucking payback time. 01:59:41 PM

Problem is, I'm not entirely sure you can build an airplane out of the shit in my motherfucking crawlspace. FUCK YOU, INACCESSIBLE CLOUDS. 02:01:37 PM

Penny Pritzker's Golden Karaoke

Snow stopped, week's done, MOTHERFUCKING BEER O'CLOCK, BITCHES. 05:00:20 PM

Karaoke in the igloo tonight. Shit's gonna get fucking nuts. Penny Pritzker's bringing her golden karaoke machine. 06:50:19 PM

Axelrod shotgunned a beer and launched right into "Hot Blooded." Motherfucking karaoke night rules. 07:08:40 PM

Carl the Intern is absolutely fucking killing it on "Tiny Dancer." He said it was for someone special. I wonder who that is? 07:35:01 PM

Axelrod. Pritzker. "Islands in the Stream." That is what they motherfucking are. 07:58:00 PM

Everyone's cheering and telling me to and I'm just playing it fucking coy. Then I grab the mic and yell, "DO YOU KNOW WHERE YOU ARE??" 08:17:22 PM

"YOU'RE IN THE MOTHERFUCKING JUNGLE, BABY!" And let me tell you, from that point on, this igloo is on fucking fire. 08:18:57 PM

We're all singing and I'm up on Axelrod's shoulders and my head is scraping against the snow ceiling, and I don't fucking care. 08:23:58 PM

This whole fucking world can lick "MY, MY, MY SERPENTINE!" 08:27:39 PM

Quaxelrod is quacking his way through motherfucking "No Sleep Till Brooklyn." Honestly, the verses are tripping him up a little. 08:41:47 PM

Penny's going solo on Cee Lo's "Fuck You," and she's amazing. Take that, Gwyneth—you fucking ruined "Glee" forever. 08:52:26 PM

Axelrod just stood up, poured a little out for dead homies, and started singing "Every Rose Has Its Thorn." A-fucking-mazing. 09:06:05 PM

And now we're all singing "Power of Love," arms clasped around each other's necks, and fuck all of you assholes, I fucking love my friends. 09:23:32 PM

Surf the Igloo!

Saturday, February 12, 2011

28 degrees? HOLY FUCK, IT'S SUMMERTIME. 08:11:11 AM

This is the first motherfucking morning in a hundred years where I'm not going to end up frozen to a commuter while shaking hands at the L. 08:24:58 AM

Summer loving: We're grilling the fucking coffee this morning. Hickory motherfucking smoked. 08:31:06 AM

29 degrees now? This bitch breaks above freezing, and we're hitting the fucking beach. 09:24:15 AM

THIRTY MOTHERFUCKING THREE DEGREES. WE FUCKING MADE IT, CHICAGO! 10:20:10 AM

■ ■ ■

Huh. This whole "living in an igloo" thing is about to get super fucking wet, isn't it? 02:10:32 PM

I ate a fucked-up chicken salad sandwich today, and I've been dealing with my own personal mayoral runoff ever since. 07:30:04 PM

Sunday, February 13, 2011

HOLY FUCK: We have achieved near-total structural failure of this motherfucking igloo. Abandon goddamn ship. 08:38:13 AM

> The temperature was close to 50 degrees, and the massive piles of snow from the blizzard two weeks before started to melt in earnest.

We're fucking surfing the remains of the igloo. You served us well, our cold, snowy friend. 08:56:44 AM

■ ■ ■

It's absolutely fucking incredible outside. Axelrod's busted out the Speedo, and we're all motherfucking jealous. 12:27:59 PM

Seriously, if you're not outside right now, you're clearly a fucking asshole. 12:41:55 PM

We are grilling every motherfucking thing we can get our hands on. Come over, it's fucking awesome. 02:31:36 PM

We pulled a Slip 'n Slide up from the crawlspace. Wet and wild, motherfuckers! Best fucking day ever. 03:10:42 PM

Quaxelrod is soaring around this beautiful blue fucking sky. He's as free as a bird now. 03:23:56 PM

■ ■ ■

Fuck you, sun! Don't fucking set on us, you fucking gas-bastard. 04:38:00 PM

■ ■ ■

Our Grammy party got ruined when we remembered that the Grammys are motherfucking awful. 08:32:34 PM

We're cleaning a few dozen cans worth of pork 'n' beans off the floor of the crawlspace. Escaped in such a hurry last week, we fucking forgot. 08:41:12 PM

Hambone, it should be said, is in fucking heaven. That little dog has probably eaten six cans' worth himself. What could go wrong with that? 08:43:37 PM

True Romance

Monday, February 14, 2011

Carl the Intern's Valentine's surprise was to dye the coffee red. It looks like we're fucking drinking blood. 07:47:10 AM

Axelrod's fucking into the blood-coffee. "It's like I'm Edward." 07:48:39 AM

That would be Edward Cullen, the vampire protagonist of the runaway hit young adult novel *Twilight*.

I'm trying to track down a bouquet of nobody-gives-a-fuck for Braun. Fuck me if the florists aren't swamped. 07:57:37 AM

There's a motherfucking debate on Valentine's Day? How fucking romantic. 08:25:28 AM

Couldn't find the flowers for Braun. Settled for a box of in-two-weeks-everyone's-going-to-fucking-forget-about-you-again. 08:34:25 AM

Valentine for Chico: On the front is a kitty holding a paper heart. Inside it says, "Let's go, asshole. Fuck you, Rahm." 08:42:02 AM

I keep starting a card for Del Valle, and then I get about 8% done and wonder why I'm even fucking bothering. 09:00:14 AM

Del Valle's poll numbers stayed consistently in the 6–8% range throughout the race.

■ ■ ■

Debate prep: Axelrod's Chico; Carl the Intern in my wife's wedding dress is Braun; Hambone is Del Valle. Quaxelrod? Carol fucking Marin. 03:23:47 PM

Carol Marin is the long-ruling queen of Chicago television news. She was the coanchor of the legendary local NBC news team in the 1980s (seriously, it was a thing) and continued her reign until 1997, when she resigned in protest because the station announced that they had signed 1990s shock-TV personality Jerry Springer as a regular commentator.

To be honest, the duck is kicking all of our asses with these fucking questions. 03:28:41 PM

Quaxelrod is clearly angling for a news anchor gig, with all his feathered fucking showboating on these debate prep questions. 04:00:29 PM

Fuck this, I'm prepped. How hard can it be: schools, budget, cops, how fucking crazy Braun is. Done, done, done, and done. 04:21:40 PM

■ ■ ■

OK, Carol Marin, let's motherfucking debate this shit. 07:02:36 PM

Next debate, we should do this shit with motherfucking Muppets. Del Valle would look incredible. 07:07:17 PM

Braun's zombie smile is fucking incredible. When I'm mayor, I'm appointing her to the committee of motherfucking crazy smiles. 07:13:51 PM

Basic debate strategy: Sit back and let everyone else motherfucking destroy each other. Chico Tea Party endorsement, go! 07:19:32 PM

> Because each non-Rahm candidate's strategy was now to be the runner-up and go to the runoff, there was a lot of undercutting one another in this debate. Most notably, out of the gate, was Miguel Del Valle referencing the fact that the Chicago Tea Party (it actually exists) had endorsed Chico. Chico's response? "Happy Valentine's Day, Miguel." Chico said he had neither sought nor knew anything about the endorsement.

So far Quaxelrod's prep questions were spot-fucking on. My "gotcha" should be about bread crumbs in the parks. Fucking ready. 07:22:13 PM

Motherfucking motherfuck, that question had nothing to do with motherfucking bread crumbs. My ass hurts. 07:24:32 PM

> Indeed, the question was not about bread crumbs but instead a pointed question about Emanuel's position on the board of directors of mortgage giant Freddie Mac from 2000 to 2001. Freddie Mac was taken over by the government following the housing market crash of the late 2000s.

I hope Jody Weis isn't doing his normal Monday-night drinking game on his name, because he's fucking gone by now. 07:35:06 PM

Police Superintendent Jody Weis was not a popular figure in the waning days of the Daley administration. During the debate, Marin raised the point that crime had gone down the past year, and why should Weis be fired?—something all the candidates had said they'd do.

You know what's pathetic? That 70% of this debate is about corruption. Motherfucking Chicago, you're a hard fucking city to love sometimes. 07:42:49 PM

■ ■ ■

Fucking goddamn done with that bullshit. VALENTINE'S NIGHT COMMENCE. 07:56:22 PM

Drinking the Carol Marin: bourbon, lemon syrup, bitters, sparkling wine. Delicious, and it'll kick your fucking ass. 08:01:37 PM

Fun fact: When my identity was revealed, I got a voicemail from Carol Marin, calling to thank me for naming a drink after her. "Now I know how Harvey Wallbanger felt."

Sufficiently drunk to move on to the highlight of my Valentine's night: throwing chunks of slush into the fucking lake. 08:15:40 PM

50 Wards in 50 Hours

Tuesday, February 15, 2011

Motherfucking coffee, you're all I fucking need today. 07:58:53 AM

50 Wards, 50 hours. Whoever the fuck thought of this is most definitely going on the cock-punch list. 09:05:59 AM

In an ambitious stunt a week out from election day, Emanuel set off to visit all 50 wards in Chicago in two days. His social media team (who were largely slow-on-the-draw through the campaign) live-tweeted the visits. I had the day off, so I set my phone to text me when the actual Emanuel account tweeted, and I would respond with a fantasy ward stop in real time.

I just visited my hundredth motherfucking L stop. One fucking week more of this shit and then all the pain goes away. 09:26:07 AM

This would be a lot more tolerable if it was 50 wards in 50 minutes. Just gun the fucking Civic and fly through all of them. 09:33:22 AM

Upside of this fucking 50 Wards concept: Pretty much every goddamn stop is a coffee shop. 50 motherfucking cups, let's go. 09:53:46 AM

Another upside: can really flesh out my "Wards that are pieces of shit" list. 10:05:27 AM

Quaxelrod's giving me fucking grief about the lack of ponds in every ward. There's a motherfucking lake—appreciate that. 10:26:14 AM

It would be motherfucking awesome if we weren't changing a tire in front of an old folks' home in the 40th Ward right now. 10:39:39 AM

That's it, it's time for a Ward-off. 44 surrounded me with adorable children. The fuck you got, 36? 11:09:19 AM

Got word that the 20th Ward has built a pit filled with fun-sized candy bars for me to jump in. Fucking top that, 27th. 11:30:14 AM

Jackpot: petting zoo in the 43rd Ward! You are so fucking fucked, 34th. 11:35:50 AM

MOTHERFUCKING BABY GOAT ALERT. Holy fuck, it's so goddamn cute it hurts. 11:42:22 AM

It's no baby goats, but the 42nd Ward had a pretty good comeback: They're all giving me piggyback rides. Fucking amazing! 11:50:47 AM

Holy shit, Ward 26—a human-sized Italian beef. I'm getting motherfucking dipped! 01:03:20 PM

> The Italian beef sandwich—invented in Chicago in the 1930s— features thin-sliced roast beef and is either served "wet" or "dry." If you order it wet, the entire sandwich is dipped in beef broth.

Word has it that the 35th has set up a miniature Tokyo and has a big Godzilla suit for me to stomp it all with. Can't fucking wait! 01:11:04 PM

Prize to the first ward that will just let me lie down and take a fucking nap. Maybe push the bed around a little, sing a song. 01:15:35 PM

Hot air balloon in the 22nd ward. I can see motherfucking Joliet from up here! 01:36:30 PM

Bumper boats in the 24th ward. You're in the motherfucking drink, Axelrod! 02:01:32 PM

Holy fuck: the 28th Ward stole all the remaining snow from the 24th and built a huge luge run! LUGE MOTHERFUCKERS, LUGE! 02:35:55 PM

Holy fuck, we're dragging that muffler down the motherfucking street, aren't we? I see fucking sparks out the back window. 03:16:08 PM

Thanks, 29th Ward, for fixing our muffler! Too bad the 31st Ward just smoked your fucking ass with a block-long banana split. 03:33:10 PM

Driving around these wards would be a whole lot fucking less boring if the goddamn radio in Axelrod's Civic wasn't busted. 04:49:36 PM

I swear to fucking god, I will donate $2,500 to the charity of your choice if you can come and fix this motherfucking radio. 05:30:31 PM

> Prior to this Tweet, the @MayorEmanuel @reply stream exploded with news that the real Rahm Emanuel had gone on a popular drive-time radio show and offered $2,500 to the charity of the author of @MayorEmanuel's choice. To say that that freaked me out would be the understatement of the year.

Ward 39 made a motherfucking mashed potato Sears Tower. It even has working elevators. Fucking incredible! 05:44:25 PM

The next motherfucking ward I visit had better have a fucking swimming pool filled with whiskey. 06:04:01 PM

Ward 41 came through with a motherfucking gin Jacuzzi. Haven't sat in one of these since Thanksgiving at Ari's. 06:33:10 PM

. . .

Hide-and-seek in the crawlspace. I am stuffed so far into this fucking box of baby clothes that nobody is ever going to find me. 08:22:09 PM

I can hear them calling my name out there, but fuck it. I can lie stiller than the fucking lake on a windless night. 08:25:45 PM

There're a couple of picture books in this box if I get bored. And a big fucking stack of cloth diapers, so I'm good on that end too. 08:28:54 PM

But here's the thing: I could stay in this box all fucking night, and you know who I am at the end of it? An asshole in a box. 08:33:04 PM

So really, what the fuck was the point of getting into this goddamn box in the first place? Oh, right: because it's a motherfucking game. 08:36:08 PM

So you fucking play the game the way it's played, right? Isn't that the whole motherfucking point of hide-and-seek: to not be found? 08:42:44 PM

Fuck it: HIDE-AND-SEEK, MOTHERFUCKERS. I'll get out of this goddamn box of baby clothes when I'm motherfucking ready. 08:47:12 PM

Which, admittedly, might be kind of soon because I think I just heard Axelrod pop a fucking beer. 08:51:54 PM

> This entire hide-and-seek section, as well as the extended hallucination sequence to come, was a reaction to Emanuel's radio appearance. While he'd specified that the money would be a charitable donation, it didn't take long for the headlines to read, simply, "Rahm Emanuel Puts a Bounty on His Twitter Imposter." And then, it suddenly felt like the search was seriously *on.*

Follow the White Rabbit

Wednesday, February 16, 2011

Fell asleep inside this box. Have the worst fucking crick in my back and can't really move. Uh, Axelrod? Carl? Hambone? Quaxelrod? Anyone? 07:22:33 AM

There was a shift in the night, and there's something on top of this box now. I can't get it open. Fucking trapped. With no coffee. 07:30:29 AM

Everyone else must be on day two of my wards tour. Which maybe is a blessing, because today is all the shitty wards. Looking at you, 14th. 07:36:04 AM

But really, there are only so many times a guy can read "Pat the Bunny," and this pile of cloth diapers is getting fucking short. 07:40:15 AM

> My son isn't a baby anymore and I was actually walking to work while I was typing this section, and *Pat the Bunny* was the only baby book I could think of. As it turned out, moments after I typed it I realized that the white rabbit on the cover would play very nicely into both an *Alice in Wonderland* and *The Matrix* reference.

I am so motherfucking hungry that I might eat this motherfucking jar of fermented baby food I found. 08:02:31 AM

Ate it. And holy fucking fuck, I swear to god the bunny on the cover of that book just winked at me. 08:07:50 AM

OK, nobody fucking panic, but this box is definitely getting fucking bigger. 08:12:21 AM

I remember packing this box, but I don't remember fitting an entire field of fucking wheat in here. That's what I'm standing in. 08:17:32 AM

Someone just ran by me in this wheat field. He was running fucking fast. All I saw was the number 34. *Sweetness?* 08:21:59 AM

Definitely Sweetness. He ran by again, this time with Pat the Bunny on his back. The fucking bunny turned and said, "Follow me."
08:25:32 AM

I have the distinct fucking feeling that this is going to be a long motherfucking day. 08:26:50 AM

■ ■ ■

We've been running through this wheat field for fucking hours now. It's so hot, I ripped a sleeve off my shirt to wipe away the sweat.
12:03:00 PM

We've reached a clearing, and Sweetness turns and says, "We're here." It's a huge motherfucking tower made out of dibs chairs.
12:05:47 PM

That fucking bunny hops off Payton's back and scampers up the tower, and Sweetness turns and says, "We've run together as far as we can." 12:08:23 PM

I turn and say, "I don't know what to do," but Sweetness is already gone, the dulcet tones of the Super Bowl Shuffle all that's fucking left. 12:10:38 PM

Well, it's either walk back through that field of wheat or climb up this tower of dibs furniture. Motherfuck it, let's head up. 12:15:02 PM

■ ■ ■

I'm probably a mile up this motherfucking tower of milk crates and lawn chairs. All I can see in every direction is wheat ringed by water. 02:30:23 PM

I've reached a landing, though the tower still fucking rises above. A door opens, and the disembodied head of Marshall Field floats out.
02:35:55 PM

Marshall Field was one of the captains of industry of turn-of-the-century Chicago. He was the owner of the Marshall Field's department store (which still stands, though it is now a Macy's), and endowed the Field Museum of Natural History, which is named after him.

You know what? Field may be a motherfucking disembodied head, but he still looks fucking classy. Dapper tie dangling down. 02:41:27 PM

Field's fucking luminescent mouth opens and he speaks: "If you want to run this city, there's some things you need to know." 02:49:51 PM

"This city burned once. The screams still haunt me. But my friends and I built it back." His head is floating fucking circles around me. 02:53:34 PM

> The Chicago Fire, which started on October 8, 1871, and burned for two days, destroyed four square miles of the city. Though the fire has long been attributed to a cow kicking over a lantern, current historians have discounted that as urban legend.

"The river, it used to bubble with poison. It killed scores. My friends and I, we reversed it." I'm getting fucking dizzy. 02:57:34 PM

> The south branch of the Chicago River used to be nicknamed the "bubbly creek" because of the gasses escaping from entrails dumped into the river from the Stock Yards in the 1800s. Add to that the fact that the sewers emptied into the river as well, and you had a very polluted waterway. The river also emptied into the lake, which is what Chicago uses for its drinking water. So you've got a problem. In 1900 engineers permanently reversed the flow of the river. Think about *that*.

"At the end of all that horror, we built a city of dreams, my friends and I. They said we couldn't. We did." I'm going to be fucking sick. 03:01:31 PM

> The World's Columbian Exposition of 1893 featured a dreamlike landscape culminating in "the White City," so-named because of the white plaster used to cover the temporary buildings. The time frame for construction of the massive undertaking was brief and many didn't believe the fairgrounds would be completed on time. The Exposition also underscored a Chicago–New York rivalry that continues to this day. In 1889, the *Chicago Tribune* wrote, "the hawks, buzzards, vultures, and other unclean beasts, creeping, crawling, and flying, of New York are reaching out to get control of the fair."

"It's a city that doesn't quit. It's a city that never stops believing." And he's humming some fucking tune I can't place. 03:10:15 PM

And I can feel myself passing out when Marshall Field floats right up to me, looks me in the fucking eyes and says: "He's looking for you." 03:13:09 PM

WHAT THE MOTHERFUCKING FU . . . 03:14:12 PM

■ ■ ■

..CK. I blacked out there. My motherfucking head is pounding. There's that fucking bunny again, climbing ever upward. Here we go. 05:00:09 PM

We're up above the clouds now. Looking down on just a sea of pink fluff. Actually, it looks motherfucking delicious. 05:05:55 PM

It's motherfucking beautiful up here, the sun making this tower of junk glow with the righteous power of millions of saved parking spaces. 05:09:39 PM

I've climbed up to another landing. Up here, the motherfucking heart of Studs Terkel is shining like a fucking beacon. 05:15:38 PM

Studs Terkel was a journalist and historian who transformed the oral history as a storytelling device through groundbreaking works like *Division Street: America; Hard Times: An Oral History of the Great Depression;* and *Working: People Talk About What They Do All Day and How They Feel About What They Do.* He died in his home in 2008. He was 96 years old.

A figure walks in front of the heart, its bright light still filtering through his translucent form. "Thumbs up, my friend." Siskel! 05:19:38 PM

Gene Siskel's smile competes with the light of Studs' heart. His thumbs are fucking enormous. 05:21:36 PM

Gene Siskel was a movie critic for the *Chicago Tribune* who is best known as the cohost of *At the Movies* with *Chicago Sun-Times* critic Roger Ebert. He died in 1999 of complications from surgery to remove a brain tumor.

He's floating just slightly above the ground, but Siskel speaks with fucking gravity: "Studs' heart beats for all Chicagoans." 05:25:35 PM

"Their shoulders are broad, but their hearts are fragile. You have to feel the pulse of the city," and he waves me towards the fucking heart. 05:26:46 PM

I'm hugging the glowing fucking heart of Studs Terkel, and it's wet and it's bright, and I can feel all of you beat inside it. 05:28:29 PM

And now Siskel is trying to pull me away with his giant fucking thumbs, but I want to stay holding this glowing heart forever. 05:31:57 PM

"We don't have much time." Siskel's yanking me backwards now, and my chest feels fucking hollow as he does it. 05:34:01 PM

"Look, there's something you need to know, about you. About this . . ." but my eyes are fucking blurred, and I can feel myself falling. 05:35:42 PM

■ ■ ■

Landed. And I'm in a white room, and there's music playing softly. And there's no wheat, and no dibs tower. There's no fucking anything. 07:13:21 PM

And out of the wall, just right there out of it, like it didn't exist at all, walks Curtis Mayfield. He's wearing a beautiful fucking suit. 07:17:37 PM

Curtis Mayfield was a seminal Chicago soul singer and performer. His work, first as a member of The Impressions, and later as a solo artist, was instrumental in defining the Chicago Soul sound.

And he's singing, really quietly, but it's beautiful. A slow version of "It's All Right." And I close my eyes, and I know that it is. 07:18:54 PM

And he's putting his hand on my arm, the one that has the sleeve missing, and for the first time in fucking months, I just feel calm. 07:20:07 PM

And the Pat the Bunny bunny comes running over, and hops into my arms. And he's so motherfucking soft, I could pat him forever. 07:22:06 PM

And Curtis is just humming now and the bunny is so fucking soft. And you know what, if this is it, this is pretty fucking good. 07:22:58 PM

But then Curtis says, in that beautiful fucking voice of his, "This isn't the kind of story where it turns out you're dead." 07:28:28 PM

"You've got a lot of life still ahead of you. Especially if you don't eat old shit you find in a box." Curtis, fucking right on on that one. 07:30:08 PM

"And there are a lot more stories still to tell. Just don't tell them with cheap-ass 'they were all dead' endings." I fucking won't, Curtis. 07:32:01 PM

"But my brother, it's not life, or stories, that I want to talk about. It's my city. It's Chicago." I'm starting to feel fucking woozy again. 07:33:43 PM

"Chicago is hurting. I can feel it," and he opens his suit and inside is no body, but the motherfucking skyline itself. 07:36:11 PM

And Curtis Mayfield points to the fucking skyline inside his chest and he says, "It needs someone, someone to hold it, someone to love it." 07:38:16 PM

And suddenly Curtis is singing again, just slow and low, and I can fucking feel the dance come back to me, and then we're dancing together. 07:39:21 PM

And then Curtis leans in really fucking close and, in a whisper, he says, "There's something else you should know, man." 07:41:55 PM

And he stops dancing and looks right at me and says, so quietly it's almost fucking inaudible, "He's looking for you." 07:43:56 PM

And I can't even ask "who" before he says, "You have to go, man. You have to go right now." And I can feel myself being pulled away . . . 07:45:21 PM

And I'm flying backwards fucking fast, but I hear Curtis yell out "NOTHING IS WHAT IT SEEMS, MAN. WHAT IF YOU'RE NOT YOU?" 07:47:06 PM

Axelrod and Carl the Intern are pulling me out of the box. "We heard you screaming from the 19th Ward." I love my fucking friends. 07:54:59 PM

Final Debate

Thursday, February 17, 2011

Today, coffee is a steaming cup of fucking awesome. 07:28:41 AM

All day prep for the final debate tonight on a hangover from hell.
Someone keep the coffee motherfucking coming. 08:35:09 AM

■ ■ ■

An entire morning of prepping for an ass fucking of a debate. Every
candidate's last chance to get a shot in. Fuck me. 12:05:15 PM

I swear to fucking god, the prep in the afternoon may as well just be
"Fight Club" style: free fucking hits, come and get 'em. 12:06:48 PM

Axelrod thought that sounded like a good idea, and just took a swing
at me. So I'll be the candidate onstage with a shiner. 12:10:25 PM

Debate prep: how to deflect all oncoming assaults from other
candidates, up to and including being set on fire. Stop, drop and
fucking roll. 12:19:51 PM

Debate prep: if I'm challenged to a motherfucking duel, do it with
swords, not pistols. 12:23:38 PM

Debate prep: if it turns into a running race, my size gives me a
distinct advantage in the 50 and 100. Distance may be a fucking
problem. 12:27:55 PM

Debate prep: in a pickup game, if it looks like Chico's going in for
a dunk, it's better to draw the foul by throwing a fucking elbow.
12:31:10 PM

Debate prep: if we end up in a dance-off, those other
motherfuckers are fucking done. "Black Swan," bitches! 12:33:01 PM

Debate prep: if someone wheels in that Jeopardy-playing computer,
I've got a motherfucking hammer at the ready. 01:06:47 PM

Watson, the *Jeopardy!*-playing computer, had just finished routing *Jeopardy!* master Ken Jennings the day before. Upon losing, Ken Jennings (who was famous for winning 74 games in a row) wrote on his *Jeopardy!* screen, "I, for one, welcome our new computer overlords."

Holy shit, have you been outside yet? It's fucking warm! Let's do the debate outside, pool-party style. 03:31:13 PM

It brushed up against 60 degrees that day. It felt incredible.

Jesus fucking Christ, it's fucking nuts with puddles out here.
06:20:48 PM

■ ■ ■

Who thought inviting 2,000 people to this last debate was a good idea? Might as well have built the fucking Thunderdome.
06:37:31 PM

The final debate was held at the Oriental Theater in Chicago's Loop Theater District. It was hosted by Ron Magers, the other coanchor of the legendary 1980s Channel 5 news team. A no-joke personal hero of mine when I was in middle school (I was a news geek from a very young age), I embarrassingly misspelled his name throughout the original Tweets—that wrong has now been righted.

Also, it's fucking disappointing that the League of Women Voters isn't going to let us come in with pyro and entrance music. What the fuck. 06:41:25 PM

I'm walking around backstage, just headfaking the fuck out of everyone. 06:49:51 PM

Wait a second—Del Valle has a motherfucking ventriloquist's dummy . . . nobody told me there was a fucking talent portion!
06:53:00 PM

OK, bitches. Let's debate this shit. This shit is so fucking ON.
07:01:14 PM

She might be completely motherfucking crazy, but Braun's new haircut is fierce. 07:05:02 PM

Hambone is still fucking pissed at me for the dog grooming tax. He's been getting extra walks to make up for it. 07:09:22 PM

> One of the budgetary proposals Emanuel put forth in the campaign was a sales tax increase on certain items, including limousine rides and pet grooming. Chico seized on this and called it the "Rahm Tax."

I am still 100% fucking positive that this debate would be way fucking better if we were using Muppets. 07:15:27 PM

I'm working on a sudoku when the camera's off me, and Jesus fucking Christ, it's making me fucking nuts. 07:21:54 PM

Oh good, we've reached the "everyone shit on Rahm" part of the debate. It's cool, I'll go get my motherfucking raincoat. 07:35:52 PM

I'm so glad I'm wearing my unicorn T-shirt under this suit. When I get down, I just think of that golden fucking horn, and I feel better. 07:39:33 PM

I want to hire Del Valle to read me bedtime stories. He opens his mouth and a motherfucking Therm-a-Rest mattress comes out. 07:47:52 PM

If a casino actually ends up in Chicago, I swear to god, I'll never see Axelrod again. Slot fucking jockey. 07:49:35 PM

> The question of locating a casino in the Chicago area had raged ever since riverboat casinos were introduced to Illinois in 1991. It came up again at this debate. Emanuel came out in favor of it.

Of all the debates I've been to, I think that Ron Magers, Captain Boring, and Fake Arianna Huffington are doing a pretty fucking good job. 07:52:33 PM

> Joining Magers were journalists Charles Thomas from ABC 7 and Paula Gomez of Univision.

LAST DEBATE OF THE MOTHERFUCKING RACE, I MADE YOU MY BITCH. 07:59:17 PM

Ron Magers, motherfucking beer me. 08:00:05 PM

Escape from Wisconsin

Axelrod and I just loaded up the Civic with beer. We're heading out to Rockford to fucking party with the exiled Wisconsin Democrats. 08:50:39 PM

> Geography lesson: Due north of Chicago is the great state of Wisconsin. Civics lesson: In Wisconsin the newly elected Republican governor announced that he was going to end all collective bargaining for state employee unions. Because there was also a newly elected Republican majority in the statehouse, this was going to pass. Bad-ass lesson: Democratic Senators realized that they could stop this vote from passing simply by not showing up for work, so there wasn't a 3–6 quorum in the Senate. So they left. Left the state. Early reports had them at a resort in Rockford, Illinois, called the Clock Tower Inn, so I sent @MayorEmanuel out to party with them.

Holy shit, Rockford sucks. But these Wisconsin Dems are fucking awesome. Beer bongs and water slides, bitches. 09:25:20 PM

Hey Wisconsin, fuck you for winning the Super Bowl, but your motherfucking Senators are bad-ass. 10:27:56 PM

Feingold just showed up with a case of whiskey and a couple of pool noodles. This motherfucking party's going all night. 10:39:05 PM

Axelrod fucking owns this water slide. He's fucking up there, calling out types of cheeses, and sending senators flying down. "Fontina!" 10:47:27 PM

Water slides, Feingold, beer brats, whiskey, and some motherfucking crazy-ass Wisconsin senators. I FUCKING LOVE MY LIFE. 10:57:41 PM

The Final Countdown

Friday, February 18, 2011

Choking down coffee in a Mobil station on the way back from Rockford. It's like drinking motherfucking rotgut. 07:29:32 AM

Up all night last night and this coffee is not fucking helping at all. Five more days of this motherfucking campaign. 07:33:36 AM

Holy fuck, by the end of this weekend my shaking hand might just fall clean off. 09:11:09 AM

■ ■ ■

In strategy sessions all morning. It's four fucking days, people; how hard can it be? Show up places, shake hands, don't be an ass. 11:41:23 AM

Axelrod shot down my plan: greet voters in a little booth under The Bean, because shit looks fucking CRAZY down there. 11:55:19 AM

> "The Bean" is the popular nickname for the Anish Kapoor sculpture *Cloud Gate*, which is the centerpiece of Millennium Park, the $475 million park Mayor Daley built. It's called The Bean because it looks like a giant mirrored lima bean. And really, when you go underneath it, it looks *crazy*.

He also won't let me hang a tire swing from the Hancock Building or sleep in the dolphin tank at the Shedd. Four days of fucking suck. 11:58:14 AM

5:00! Motherfucking Friday fucking night starts right goddamn now. 04:59:56 PM

■ ■ ■

HOLY FUCK, THE MOON IS MOTHERFUCKING ENORMOUS. 07:04:58 PM

> While the "supermoon"—the closest the moon would be to the earth in 18 years—was actually supposed to shine the next night, it was equally huge that night.

Saturday, February 19, 2011

I am the motherfucking donut king this morning. 08:42:53 AM

OK, you sunny, chilly Saturday, prepare to get fucked. 09:26:35 AM

With all the snow melted, it takes Hambone about an hour to make it around one fucking block because of the mountains of shit he can sniff. 09:34:48 AM

> Having had a dog in Chicago for many years, I can confirm that this was a familiar experience—weeks and weeks of dog shit, all exposed at once after a big melt.

This city is at its absolute ugliest when the snow melts. Fucking drifts of weeks-old Cheetos bags and Snickers wrappers. 09:55:23 AM

■ ■ ■

Motherfucking canoe races in Washington Park. Quaxelrod is smoking everyone's ass. 01:15:34 PM

Girl Scouts on Cottage Grove! I am going to fuck up this box of Samoas! 02:54:17 PM

Jesus fucking Christ, Samoa crash. I can't even fucking move. 03:12:29 PM

Sunday, February 20, 2011

Coffee! You are motherfucking wonderful! Let me carry you gently in my goddamn belly! 08:06:17 AM

Carl the Intern has been training a legion of volunteers this week. Chicago, prepare to get motherfucking hang-tagged. 08:38:17 AM

Carl calls them The InternCorps; they're all wearing these fucking green rings. "We'll be fine, as long as Chico's not wearing yellow." 08:48:49 AM

> The Green Lantern Corps, an intergalactic police force featured in the DC Comics universe, uses green power rings that are essentially omnipotent, except against the color yellow. For real.

Holy shit, the crawlspace is flooding! MOTHERFUCK YOU RAIN! 09:35:53 AM

> With the melted snow saturating the ground, the additional inch of rain that fell caused a fair amount of flooding in the region.

Spent the morning bailing out the crawlspace. Our sleeping bags are fucking soaked. Just fucking perfect. 10:51:28 AM

Quaxelrod's fucking loving it though, bobbing his way around all the board games and action figures floating around down there. 10:59:30 AM

Lynn Sweet thinks she's being cute publishing that old photo of me in a leotard. MOTHERFUCKING DANCE OFF, LYNN. LET'S GO. 11:12:06 AM

> *Chicago Sun-Times* political reporter Lynn Sweet published a photo
> Sunday morning of Rahm Emanuel, in a leotard with a sweet Jewfro.
> She actually responded to this Tweet, saying "Danceoff? When? Please
> tweet a reply that does not have the F word in it so i can retweet to my
> followers . . ." @MayorEmanuel complied with her request: "You don't
> want to mess with the black swan, bitch." Not a single F-word.

■ ■ ■

Lunch with the Jesse White Tumblers. This gray fucking day just got a whole lot brighter. 12:34:32 PM

It's too wet to tumble outside, so the Tumblers have set up their mats and springboard here in the motherfucking restaurant. Yes! 01:03:20 PM

The Tumblers are fucking amazing, flying right over the people eating. Each flip brings them closer to the ceiling. Beautiful! 01:24:39 PM

Now everyone's fucking cheering—Jesse White, the Tumblers, the people eating—and one of the Tumblers calls out, "The runway's all yours!" 01:31:05 PM

And everyone's cleared the way, made a space for me to run at the fucking springboard. And now I'm running as fast as I can. 01:35:21 PM

AND I'M FLYING THROUGH THE AIR AND I WISH THIS MOMENT COULD LAST FOR FUCKING EVER. 01:37:43 PM

And I hit the mat and stick the landing and everyone's cheering except Jesse White, who just gives me this awesome fucking two-finger point. 01:44:30 PM

Two more motherfucking days of this campaign, and if flying through the air free as a bird is the best there is, well I'll fucking take it. 01:56:36 PM

Now let's go dump some fucking Chico signs in potholes brimming with dogshit-infused rainwater runoff. 02:04:09 PM

■ ■ ■

Duct-taped a TV to the ceiling of the crawlspace and found some pool floats to sleep on. It's like living inside a fucking waterbed: amazing. 08:23:01 PM

We're just bobbing around in this flooded crawlspace flipping between repeats of Martin and news from motherfucking Wisconsin. 08:37:35 PM

> Protesters in Wisconsin, still angry over the attempt to end collective bargaining, had taken over the Capitol Rotunda.

And maybe it's the fucking beer talking, but I see those shots from inside the fucking rotunda, and I just get weepy. 08:41:38 PM

I mean, yeah, all those people are fucked, but they're going to fucking go down fighting. Also important: Martin Lawrence is hilarious. 08:43:41 PM

Also: we've got our beer down under the floodwater, and Quaxelrod dives down when we need new cans. Ice fucking cold. 08:45:23 PM

Floating in my basement, watching TV with friends, drinking cold beer, 34 hours before polls open: fucking living the dream. 08:58:43 PM

The Two Mayors

Monday, February 21, 2011

Fucking shit fuck. Motherfucking overslept on the last fucking full day of campaigning. 08:06:00 AM

Hambone just brought the schedule: (1) shake 10,000 voters' hands; (2) pick up Ari from the airport; (3) keep Ari away from voters. Fuck. 08:22:17 AM

Let's just keep the motherfucking coffee coming, non-fucking stop. 08:31:06 AM

When I run for reelection, I'm having a motherfucking hand-shaking robot built. 09:01:48 AM

Carl the Intern and Axelrod are directing the InternCorps from "the command center"—a laptop and a map in the backseat of the fucking Civic. 10:02:51 AM

Asked Carl how things were going, and he said, "In brightest day, in blackest night, no evil shall escape my sight." The fuck does that mean? 10:05:58 AM

> It's the Green Lantern's oath: In brightest day, in blackest night, no evil shall escape my sight. Let those who worship evil's might, beware my power . . . Green Lantern's light!

Then he had to go running back to the Civic because Axelrod called out that "We need more Corps in sector 2814." What the fuck? 10:09:43 AM

> Sector 2814, according to DC Comics, is one of 3,600 sectors into which the Guardians of the Universe had divided the universe. It is also the sector of the universe that includes the Earth.

■ ■ ■

Fuck you, snow. Nobody fucking wants you here. Go the fuck away. 01:05:28 PM

> Another 2 to 4 inches was predicted to fall.

I've said it before, but I'll say it again: whoever thought it was a good idea to have an election in February was a fucking asshole. 02:11:55 PM

The snow's delayed Ari's plane for a couple of hours. Probably best if it were delayed until motherfucking Wednesday. 03:36:37 PM

Wrapped in a blanket while riding shotgun in the Civic on the way to get Ari from the airport. The wind is cold through the missing window. 05:18:26 PM

"Nice blanket, Linus. Fix the fucking airport once you're mayor, OK asshole?" Motherfucking Ari. My brother's here. 05:40:32 PM

"How come every news clip I see of you, you're acting like a giant walking hernia?" He's here for two fucking days. 05:54:52 PM

"I had no clue that the prerequisite for running for mayor was chopping your balls off." We're stuck in fucking stop-and-go traffic. 06:05:51 PM

"Hey, how come your fucking radio doesn't work? What kind of piece of shit car is this?" And I can see Axelrod turning red. 06:19:08 PM

"Fucking Spielberg alone gave you enough to buy a fucking Beemer, and you're driving around in this shit?" Uh-oh—Axelrod's pulling off. 06:27:42 PM

And now we're all standing outside and Axelrod's yelling "LET'S GO, ASSHOLE!" at Ari. He really loves his fucking car. 06:34:11 PM

They're down in the snow, pummeling each other. And I don't even notice the figure behind me until the bag's already over my head. Fuck. 06:41:06 PM

■ ■ ■

I'm fucking gasping when the bag comes off. We've been driving around for an hour, clearly trying to confuse me. It worked. 08:15:26 PM

I'm still blinking, and the light is grinding a migraine into being, when I hear a voice fucking boom out from above me. 08:17:42 PM

"Sorry for the drama, but it's not like I could just invite you over here for tea." My fucking eyes start to come into focus. 08:19:33 PM

I pull my head up from the marble floor and there, standing above me, is the massive fucking frame of Mayor Daley. 08:20:32 PM

Daley helps me up, his hands fucking envelop my arms completely. "Sorry again, but we needed to talk tonight. Can't take chances."
08:26:47 PM

"Look, there are some things you need to know." I'm here! In his office! In City fucking Hall! 08:28:50 PM

"So the toilet, just down the hall, you need to jiggle the handle after you flush." Daley's not really making eye contact. 08:29:50 PM

"And Magdalena, she cleans up on alternating nights. If you have shit you don't want thrown out, make sure you put it away."
08:30:40 PM

"And I've made a little calendar of all the secretaries' birthdays. Don't forget." If I didn't know better, I'd think Daley was welling up.
08:33:24 PM

And suddenly Daley's tears are gone, and they're replaced by anger. "Don't fuck all this up. There's so much more than you know." 08:37:06 PM

And Daley's gesturing for me to follow him, and suddenly we're out a window and heading up a motherfucking fire escape. 08:38:49 PM

We're on the roof of City Hall. The wind is fucking strong and the snow stings when it hits my face. Daley heads into a glass dome.
08:47:31 PM

It's so warm and beautiful in the dome—green everywhere—and the air is pungent with the smell of . . . is that fucking celery?
08:50:06 PM

> There is a garden on the roof of City Hall, originally planted in 2000 to demonstrate the benefits of green roofs. No part of the garden, to the best of my knowledge, is covered by a glass dome. There are beehives up there though, which is just very cool.

Daley fucking plucks a stalk. "Care for these. Let flowers bloom. Dry them. Harvest the seeds. Grind them. Mix with salt." 08:53:22 PM

> This is my favorite Tweet of the entire stream: the entire process of growing, harvesting, drying, and creating celery salt encapsulated in a

single Tweet. Celery salt is the key topping on a Chicago-style hot dog. It's how you know you're eating a real Chicago dog. And it's delicious.

He hands me a small pinch of powder and the sharp taste of celery salt crosses my lips. "Our legacy," he says, and points to the stalks. 08:58:18 PM

And it's then that I notice for the first fucking time that, nestled amid the stalks of celery, are three modest headstones. 08:59:54 PM

Daley points to the headstones. "They're here with us, always. Harrison, Washington, Dad." He chokes up on that last one. 09:05:11 PM

I search the ground for three small pebbles. Daley's fucking silent while I place one on each of the gravestones. 09:07:38 PM

Carter Henry Harrison was a wildly popular mayor of Chicago at the end of the 19th century. Harold Washington was the first African-American mayor of Chicago, elected in 1983. And of course Richard J. Daley was Mayor Daley's father, elected in 1955. All three died in office.

"It blooms year-round, thanks to them," he says quietly. And we're just looking, standing, breathing the thick moist air. Together. 09:10:26 PM

"There's something else." Daley breaks the silence, his voice cracking just a fucking little. He flips a switch on the wall. 09:18:49 PM

There's a whirring sound and then, up from the center of the dome, rises an oversized charcoal grill. What the fuck? 09:21:08 PM

"The mayor doesn't just run Chicago," Daley says, walking over to the grill. "You need to understand what's really at stake here." 09:24:17 PM

Daley lifts the lid of the grill, his body straining under the weight. And suddenly I don't want to fucking know what's inside. 09:28:01 PM

"There's not just one Chicago. There's not just one you. It's infinite. And we keep the portal," and he gestures for me to fucking look in. 09:31:31 PM

And I look and . . . and it's Chicago—again and again. And tiny, in the corner, peering up at me, is . . . me. Thousands. Millions. 09:36:31 PM

Except. Except something feels fucking wrong. "You notice it too," says Daley. "There's one of you missing." 09:38:32 PM

And Daley looks at me deadly fucking serious and says, "Which means there are two of you here, in this world, in this time." 09:45:45 PM

"Which means," and he looks at me now, and there are fucking tears on his face, "that one of you won't survive this election." 09:48:19 PM

And, before I can try to figure out what the fuck Daley's going on about, the bag is back on my head, and everything goes black. 09:51:14 PM

Election Day

Tuesday, February 22, 2011

HOLY FUCK, if there's any fucking day in the world that I need coffee, it is this fucking day. 07:01:51 AM

I'm drinking coffee and explaining everything that happened last night. Axelrod looks so surprised his fucking mustache might fall off. 07:05:14 AM

Carl the Intern has filled an entire fucking chalkboard with equations by the time I'm done talking. "Daley's right," is all he says. 07:11:17 AM

And when he says it, Quaxelrod lets out the saddest fucking quack-moan you've ever heard a duck make. 07:11:55 AM

"I don't know nothing about infinite fucking Chicagos," Axelrod says. "I only know this one. And polls have been open for an hour." 07:18:12 AM

Axelrod's right. Whatever the motherfucking outcome, we've got a fucking election to win. LET'S DO THIS. 07:19:34 AM

■ ■ ■

Anyone that isn't voting today because of the snow is a motherfucking asshole. Or an invalid—OK, you've got a good excuse. 09:54:01 AM

Fifteen motherfucking Get Out The Vote rallies and it's barely even noon. Might have to hold a Get Out The Nap rally later. 12:09:27 PM

■ ■ ■

Get Out The Nap was exactly what was fucking needed. Now we're driving old people to the polls. Ari's hitting on most of them. 02:33:20 PM

VOTE, BITCHES. 03:11:58 PM

Carl the Intern wrote two speeches for me, one for winning and one for a runoff. There's a lot more motherfucking profanity in the latter. 04:40:19 PM

Sitting in the backseat of Axelrod's Civic practicing these fucking speeches. Quaxelrod's giving notes. So far, he's unimpressed. 05:25:07 PM

Carl and the InternCorps are on balloon duty at the party space. Ari's over there too, rearranging fucking everything. Again. 05:25:31 PM

Axelrod and Hambone are standing outside the Civic, Hambone's taking a shit, Axelrod's checking exit polls. There's a fucking metaphor. 05:26:53 PM

Everyone's talking runoff, but I know it's a victory. My fingerstump disappeared this morning and now the rest of the hand is fucking going. 05:35:12 PM

Time to head in to start watching results. I'm wearing a single glove over my invisible hand, motherfucking MJ style. 06:11:27 PM

■ ■ ■

7:00. Here goes motherfucking nothing. 07:04:36 PM

The polls officially closed at 7 pm.

Jesus fucking Christ. Time to start fucking drinking. Axelrod—beer me! 07:07:17 PM

Axelrod's in with the early results: 51 motherfucking percent. Still a long night, but SUCK ON THAT, CHICO. 07:36:20 PM

FIFTY-FOUR MOTHERFUCKING PERCENT, BITCHES. 07:43:00 PM

The party is kicking the fuck off in the ballroom below. And I'm fucking seven beers in up here. 07:47:50 PM

CNN FUCKING CALLS IT, BITCHES. 07:49:24 PM

CNN was the first news organization to call the election for Emanuel, just 49 minutes after the polls closed. Everyone expected a long night, but this wasn't one.

These motherfucking robotic vote-counting machines are kind of fucking incredible, aren't they? 07:51:08 PM

The big plan for tonight: We've got a champagne fountain from the top of the ballroom to the stage. I'm going to fucking ride down it. 07:53:46 PM

Ari's on the mic bringing the fucking noise downstairs. Mainly just bitching out the caterers. 08:01:25 PM

Quaxelrod's already taking motherfucking a fucking victory flap around the rafters of the ballroom. 08:04:40 PM

STUPID FUCKS AT WGN CALL IT TOO. 08:08:02 PM

Twenty minutes after CNN, the local Chicago media began to call the election for Emanuel as well.

Hey, Halpin, I'll give you until the end of the fucking night to start packing. 08:09:03 PM

If you have a giant fucking pile of money and a bunch of dumb fucks running against you, DREAMS DO COME TRUE. 08:14:45 PM

Just think about how much fucking more incredible this would feel if the Bears had won the Super Bowl too. 08:27:43 PM

Carl the Intern just ran in, with a notebook full of fucking numbers, his eyes wet with tears. "The time vortex: it'll close tomorrow." 08:33:34 PM

Elected mayor tonight. Sucked into a time vortex tomorrow. Might as well KICK THIS PARTY OFF RIGHT FUCKING NOW. 08:37:10 PM

Axelrod and I are double-fisting beers, smashing the empties on our foreheads. IT FEELS FUCKING GREAT TO BE ALIVE. 08:57:48 PM

Fuck the fucking champagne slide, I'm just going to jump out of this fucking window and crowdsurf to the fucking stage. 09:00:15 PM

I'M FUCKING RIDING ON THE BODIES OF THE MEN AND WOMEN OF CHICAGO, AND I FUCKING LOVE EVERY ONE OF YOU. 09:01:55 PM

Turns out crowdsurfing your way up to a stage takes a long fucking time. OK, victory speech—let's fucking do this. 09:17:51 PM

Quaxelrod soars down from the balcony and lands gently on my shoulder. I stroke his downy fucking feathers and begin. 09:19:35 PM

"FUCK YES CHICAGO! This has been a long fucking campaign. The other assholes didn't stand a chance, but they put up a good fight." 09:25:18 PM

"The motherfuckers that contested my residency, you've got some great days ahead of you, I fucking promise you that." 09:26:16 PM

"But to the rest of you, I've talked with a fuck-ton of you and I've learned about your resiliency, about your spirit." 09:29:49 PM

"I've learned that this is Chicago and that CHICAGO DOESN'T FUCKING QUIT, NOT FUCKING EVER." 09:31:38 PM

"I've slept in an igloo and I've slept in a crawlspace and I've slept under a bridge. But as long as I was asleep in Chicago, I didn't care." 09:33:42 PM

"I've held the motherfucking pulsating heart of Chicago in my hands, and I know that it beats true." 09:35:18 PM

"Through everything—through assholes, through cockholes—I've had two things: the people of Chicago, and my fucking friends." 09:39:06 PM

"And sure, to save the fucking world, I have to disappear into a time vortex tomorrow. But being mayor is about making the hard decisions." 09:41:46 PM

"But tomorrow is tomorrow, and TONIGHT'S A FUCKING PARTY. LET'S GO CHICAGO!" 09:45:55 PM

And I dive into the crowd, and their hands hold me up, and together we are fucking one. 09:47:52 PM

This party's going to go all fucking night. Fuck you, tomorrow, you're just gonna have to wait. 11:21:47 PM

Into the Vortex

Wednesday, February 23, 2011

Motherfucking coffee, I'm going to drink you like there's no goddamn tomorrow. 07:37:08 AM

They'd better have coffee in the parallel fucking dimension I'm descending into tonight, or I'm breaking right back out. 07:45:01 AM

We're sharing a cup together in the crawlspace, and I can tell that Axelrod's trying not to cry by the way his mustache fucking quivers. 07:50:45 AM

Axelrod looks up, tears filling his eyes, and says, simply, "Don't go." Fucking time portals are a son of a bitch. 07:58:30 AM

"There must be something we can do . . ." But there's not. Only things that fucking suck never end: look at laundry, or dishes. 08:05:27 AM

And we hug, and I give Axelrod that look that asks, "Are you going to be OK?" And he gives me that look that says, "Who fucking knows?" 08:11:53 AM

And we sit down and plan out one last, perfect, day: lunch at Manny's, mooning Chico, tossing fucking bread to Quaxelrod. 08:15:10 AM

■ ■ ■

Watching Axelrod eat at Manny's is like watching Da Vinci paint the motherfucking Mona Lisa: a work of art. 12:54:27 PM

■ ■ ■

Driving around in Axelrod's Civic, doing loops around the block outside Chico's offices, my ass hanging out of the missing window, laughing. 03:16:41 PM

■ ■ ■

Tossing bread to Quaxelrod under the Cortland Street Bridge. The view from here is motherfucking incredible. 04:28:57 PM

■ ■ ■

Knowing I'm entering a time vortex tonight would be a lot more tolerable if I could get Journey's "Separate Ways" out of my fucking head. 05:44:58 PM

> If you have that track handy, queue it up now. In fact, once you're done reading, you might want to pour some coffee or grab a beer, depending on the time of day, and listen to Journey's *Greatest Hits* in its entirety, just because that would be an awesome thing to do.

Picked up Carl the Intern at Lane Tech, after his mathletes practice. Carl's first words: "There's not much time left." Motherfuck. 06:53:30 PM

We're driving down Elston when, all of a fucking sudden, Axelrod's radio starts working. It's playing that fucking Journey song!
07:02:07 PM

And we've pulled the Civic over, turned up "Separate Ways," and we're fucking dancing out here on the motherfucking streets!
07:04:44 PM

FUCK YOU, YOU MOTHERFUCKING TIME VORTEX. I FUCKING LOVE DANCING WITH MY FRIENDS. 07:07:09 PM

■ ■ ■

And then the sky fucking opens up on us, and there're chunks of ice flying down. And it's pretty clear that the party's over. 07:26:17 PM

And I can see myself starting to fade out, and I hear Axelrod whispering the fucking Kaddish quietly to himself, tears streaming. 07:31:38 PM

And that song's still playing from the car radio, on a never-fucking ending loop from hell. 07:32:45 PM

Carl the Intern can't even make eye contact, but he's reaching out, and I touch his hand. And he says, "I love you," and I say, "I know." 07:34:27 PM

Quaxelrod flies over, dips his little head, and touches my fading shoe. Hambone just curls softly between my invisible legs. 07:37:28 PM

I can see a thousand fucking skylines, and they are all as motherfucking glorious as the first, and I can feel the touch of my friends. 07:39:08 PM

And now all I can hear is that music, and suddenly everything just fucking . . . 07:40:45 PM

The Epilogue

Discovered (part one)

"You are @mayoremanuel."

It's not the kind of thing you want to see in the subject line of an e-mail when you've just pressed "send" on a Tweet that reads "Public Service Announcement: In about three hours, you're going to need a lot of fucking whiskey." It was February 1: 21 inches of snow were about to fall on Chicago, and @MayorEmanuel and his friends were preparing for a snowpocalypse. And suddenly, the gig was up.

"I'm not going to unmask you but I can tell you how to cover your tracks better," was all the e-mail said. The name was one I recognized from @MayorEmanuel's @replies—he'd been doggedly pursuing the identity of @MayorEmanuel for about a week, accusing multiple people over Twitter, with denials all around. Beyond that, I had no idea who he was. Was he press? Was he pissed? Was I done?

I responded the way I'd done in the past: "Oh man, I wish." And then I waited, stomach in my fucking throat, waiting for a response.

It came a day later, while Chicago was digging out from the massive snowstorm and after @MayorEmanuel had moved into an igloo:

> Early in the @mayoremanuel feed the user used bitl.lys. One of the first is this: http://bit.ly/cB868e+

Which you built. Only these people tweeted it:

twitter.com	95
/marcusleshock	2
/MayorEmanuel	37
/mayoremanuel	26

Where'd you put it?

I clicked on the bit.ly URL, and there, staring me in the face, was my actual name. I'd shortened a link for @MayorEmanuel when I was logged in as myself. And while I could possibly deny one, I was sure I'd done it before that as well. *He had me.* I thought I was going to throw up.

I e-mailed two of my trusted circle of friends who knew the secret. Their response:

"Who is this person?" and "Fuck."

As I saw it, I had two choices: Own up, or fruitlessly try to deny it. I swallowed, and nervously typed out a response:

> Nice work.
> Thought I'd take one more whack at denying it, but that really was great tech sleuthing. Gotta tip my hat—nobody else had even gotten close.
> Now, why would you want to ruin all this fun?

And I sat, and I waited, and I hoped.

I

Origin Stories

You don't sit down one night and say, "I'm going to write a satirical take on a mayoral race and, in the process, redefine storytelling for the real-time web, raise $13,000 for a youth writing program, and accidentally become Internet Famous."

Because if you did that, you'd be an asshole. And you'd fail.

Instead, you sit down and do something noble: you try to make your friends laugh.

That's what I did, on September 27, late at night. Rumors were swirling about the possibility of Rahm Emanuel leaving the White House to run for mayor of Chicago. It had broken in *Politico*, been reported in the *Chicago Tribune*, and was moving through Twitter the way things do: *fast*.

For reasons I wish I could remember better, a few weeks earlier I'd secured the Twitter ID @MayorEmanuel (they're free to secure, so why not). I didn't know what I'd do with it—at one point I'd toyed with writing a postapocalyptic tale of the end of the Emanuel mayoralship in a Chicago that resembled a wasteland. High concept, to be sure. It never happened.

The act of getting an idea and seeing what I could do with it is one that I'm very familiar with. I started a magazine, *Punk Planet*, at the age of 19 because I thought it might be interesting. That magazine lasted for 13 years, spun off a second, short-lived magazine (the skateboard culture mag *Bail*), and launched a line of books. I taught myself how to code websites back in 1994 because the Internet seemed like a good idea. In 2009 I launched CellStories, a web application that published works of short fiction exclusively for mobile phones, because I was interested in seeing how publishing on a mobile device would work. I really believe that you learn best when you're making things—it's even wrapped into the DNA of the college classes I teach—and so that's what I do: I get an idea, and I see where it goes.

In the case of @MayorEmanuel, *where* was here, on my couch, on September 27, 2010. I'd already registered the Twitter account and so I thought *why not*. I tweeted: "Fuck you in your fucking face-hole." I tweeted to *Politico*. To the *Tribune*. To friends who were talking about the Emanuel rumors. All of the Tweets were angry, with profanity filling much of the 140 characters allotted.

I retweeted—re-posted a Tweet on my own account—a single Tweet from @MayorEmanuel, his missive to *Politico*. That retweet got retweeted, along with the other Tweets from that night, and, surprisingly quickly, a few hundred people had started following the account. By the next day, following a few dozen more Tweets, that number had grown to around 1,000.

Honestly, it started as a way of entertaining a few people. Suddenly, it had an audience.

The Daily Grind

It's a 30-minute train ride from my house to downtown Chicago, where I work. It's another 25 minutes walking from the station to my office. That's 55 minutes, twice a day, at the same time that many other people are doing the same thing. That meant that when I was writing, people were guaranteed to be reading.

If I'd worked the night shift, or not worked at all, the times wouldn't have lined up so well. But in the 7:30 to 9:30 am window (teaching gives you some flexibility), and the reverse commute in the evening, you're guaranteed an alert audience. So that's how it started: writing for that audience: people traveling to and from work, planning the day in their head, or feeling glad it was over, on the way home. To create a story that's relatable to that audience, you do what they're doing: you complain about work:

Jesus shit-Christ, is it awkward around the office today.

That was one of the first work-related Tweets from @MayorEmanuel, sent out at 9:24 in the morning on September 28. The concept was that the leaked stories the day before would make for uncomfortable water-cooler whispers, the same way a suddenly discovered office romance would. It was a theme—the drudgery of the "job" of running for mayor—that would drive a lot of the early narrative. It introduced the main characters—David Axelrod first shows up more as a foil than a friend—and set out the basic logic of @MayorEmanuel: he knew he was going to win, and he viewed everything in between as one big pain in his ass.

We've all been there: meetings that never end, a colleague who won't let a bad idea go, the way your mind wanders away from the real work at hand. You end up hoping and praying for an opportunity like this:

> **Geithner never stops talking. You can be standing there, double birds in his face and your cock hanging out, and he's all blah blah blah . . .**

Universality is crucial in a story. I've never run for mayor. Most likely, neither have you. But I've had jobs that drove me crazy, same as you. So bringing that experience in—especially during the time that everyone's riding a train, either dreading their day or feeling exhausted from it—meant that people related, and retweeted. Hence the obsessions with coffee and Fridays.

The result? That 1,000 followers started to grow. And grow.

Being Rahm

What do you have against Rahm Emanuel?

It's a question that I've been asked many times, and an answer that, when I give, nobody believes: *not much.*

But it's true: I wasn't making fun *of* Rahm Emanuel, I was making fun *with* Rahm Emanuel.

From the moment—September 7, 2010—that Mayor Daley announced he was going to end his 21-year mayorship, it was clear that the mayoral race in Chicago was going to be two things:

1) Historic
2) A Circus

Every character in Chicago was going to make an appearance over the six months that the race would be run. Millions of dollars would be spent. Political hay would be made. As the city that works worked out who its next mayor would be, it was going to be a spectacle. A spectacle ripe for parody.

And then there was Emanuel: a longtime figure in Washington who had cultivated an air of myth around himself that centered around his foul mouth and his no-holds-barred politics. He's famous for mailing a dead fish to a pollster who pissed him off (a story he's confirmed) and for haranguing a congressperson for his vote on health-care reform naked in the congressional showers (a story he hasn't). Beyond the myth, he has been massively successful in politics. He has served as a senior advisor to President Clinton; as a congressperson from Chicago after that, where he was the chair of the Democratic Congressional Campaign Committee and later the Democratic Caucus chairman; and finally as the chief of staff to President Obama.

And yet what's most interesting to me about Emanuel isn't any of that, it's who he was before he entered politics: a dancer who worked at an Arby's Roast Beef in high school, a guy who turned down a scholarship to the prestigious Joffrey Ballet school to enroll in, of all places, Sarah Lawrence. You extend that background out and you don't expect to arrive at the person he became.

It's this juxtaposition—the liberal-arts dancer Emanuel against the dead-fish hothead—that makes Emanuel such a great character to write. Fold in the additional detail that he's a polarizing figure in politics—he's either revered or reviled, there is almost no middle ground—and you've got a perfect central figure for a story about this historic election.

There was no other candidate in the Chicago mayoral race who would have worked (lord knows it was tried—there were parody Twitter accounts set up for every candidate by the time @MayorEmanuel hit its stride, none of them long-lasting). With any other candidate, there either wasn't enough name recognition outside Chicago political circles; their backstories weren't very interesting; or it just felt mean. No, Emanuel was a perfect storm.

Plus with Emanuel, you really do get to swear, *a lot.*

Mashups

@MayorEmanuel was a voracious mashup. Everything went into his blender: *Tron. Harry Potter. Say Anything. 300. The Matrix. Star Wars. A Charlie Brown Christmas. Groundhog Day. Rushmore. Black Swan. Space Jam. Lost. Glee. Moby Dick. Oliver Twist. A Christmas Carol. Titanic.* Dungeons and Dragons. *Lord of the Rings.* The Bulls. The Bears. Guns N' Roses. Journey . . . @MayorEmanuel took all of them and combined them with politics, geography, the weather, anything. Everything.

Sometimes the nods were elaborate, like the extended homage to Luke's run-in with a Wampa in *The Empire Strikes Back,* which plays out during Bill Clinton's visit. It wasn't the only time that Chicago's Arctic temperatures had inspired a reference in the feed to the ice planet Hoth, but it was the most direct. Shivering my way home from dropping off my son at his chess club, I laughed at the idea of David Axelrod stuffing a frozen Bill Clinton inside the backseat of his Honda Civic, mirroring the way that Han Solo saves the life of a frozen Luke Skywalker. That was it: that single image led to a series of Tweets:

> Woke up and Clinton's gone! His clothes and wallet are here. He's gonna fucking freeze out there. Come back, Big Bear!

> Axelrod's going to search, but Carl the Intern said his Civic will freeze before he reaches the first marker. "Then I'll see you in hell!"

> Axelrod found him, face down in a snow bank muttering something about Ben Bernanke. Just "Ben . . . Ben . . . Ben . . ." over and over. The fuck?

> Axelrod cut open the back seat of his Civic—"I thought they smelled bad on the outside"—and stuffed Clinton inside to keep him warm.

> Now they're back and Carl the Intern's filling this big-ass tube with hot water. Sticking Clinton in there to warm him the fuck up.

> Clinton looks strong enough to pull the ears off a mother-
> fucking gundark. Axelrod says, "That's two you owe me,
> Big Bear."

> Now Axelrod and Carl the Intern are arguing and Hambone
> starts barking like crazy. Axelrod spins around and says,
> "Bark it up, fuzzball."

> And now Carl's planting a big kiss on Clinton, and he's just
> lying there hands behind his head with a big shit-eating grin.
> What the fuck?

> We gotta get Clinton back to the airport now. I don't know
> how the fuck he's going to explain that big scar on his cheek
> to Hillary.

I'll admit: I didn't know that entire scene by heart (thankfully). I had the clip cued up on YouTube so I could get the dialogue and order of the actions correct.

Sometimes the mashup was much more subtle, like the *Rushmore* reference that drops into the middle of the returns from the midterm elections:

> Hey, Meg Whitman, you can buy anything, but you can't buy
> motherfucking backbone.

The mashups became a game for @MayorEmanuel's followers—figuring out the references, guessing at the foreshadowing that might be buried inside of them (the extended references to "In Your Eyes," the Peter Gabriel song that marks the emotional climax of *Say Anything*, had a number of followers correctly predicting the ending of the week without Axelrod and Carl the Intern), even catching things that I hadn't even thought of (the glass dome on the roof of City Hall, for instance, has been compared to Ozymandias's Arctic dome in the seminal graphic novel *Watchmen*, which I've read probably a couple of dozen times but didn't intend to reference, though I was clearly influenced by that imagery).

One unintended reference came near the end of the feed: it's election day, and @MayorEmanuel has started to slowly disintegrate into time itself:

> Everyone's talking runoff, but I know it's a victory. My fingerstump disappeared this morning and now the rest of the hand is fucking going.

Tons of people in the @reply stream thought this was a *Back to the Future* reference, from the scene in which Marty McFly sees his own hand begin to disappear because he wasn't able to make his parents meet at a dance (time travel's weird like that). That wasn't intentional, but when I saw people claim the reference I knew I had an out from the corner I'd written myself into: If Emanuel hadn't won the election on February 22, there was a runoff scheduled for April 5, and I had no plan for how to reverse course from the very clear ending I'd set up. *Back to the Future* was my out: Carl the Intern could soup up Axelrod's Civic, string a wire from the Dearborn Station clock tower, and race back in time to reverse the outcome of the election, forcing a runoff. It was elaborate but, really, at that point, what wasn't?

Beyond the cross-cultural mashups that proliferated in the account, @MayorEmanuel was itself a remix: one that mashed up real-world characters with fictional ones, one that took real-world events and combined them with fantasy, and one that took the world you lived in and juxtaposed it with one in which you decidedly didn't.

Telling Stories Out of School

The mashing up of fact and fiction started small, just bending reality into a funhouse mirror of itself. You look back at the early days of the feed and that's what you see: reality, turned on its head. The "stories" in those early days are short, two or three Tweet arcs. They begin and they abruptly end. But they start to refer back to one other, actions lead to other actions. Characters begin to develop. And they start to do unexpected things:

Today was one never-ending fucking strategy session.
Workloads doubled when Axelrod's mustache announced it
was taking the week off.

Seriously, if that motherfucking 'stache is talking to fucking
Meeks, I'm going to lose it.

David says it's just taking a few days to see the fall colors
in WI, but really: what fucking mustache takes off two weeks
before midterms?

Anyway, a week without that mustache just went from a slog
to a motherfucking full-fledged shit-wallow.

I peg those four short Tweets about David Axelrod's mustache
taking the week off as the beginning of the rest of the feed—it was the
first freewheeling moment, one that didn't require external situations
to kick off the action. This was about two weeks into the life of the
feed. A few weeks after that, things really changed:

Holy fuck, I've eaten so much candy corn that I think I can
see through motherfucking time!

Caught in a fucking candy-corn haze. Jean Baptiste Point du
Sable and Papa Bear Hallas are dancing. Axelrod's mustache
sings like an angel.

John Belushi and Harold Washington are swimming in the
river. Their bodies bleed together in the dark murk of the
water. FUCKING BEAUTIFUL.

I look out the window and the Hancock and the Sears reach
out and kiss each other tenderly. My fucking tears taste like
celery salt.

The stars are red and the sky is striped with blue. I baptize
myself in the lake's frigid waters. I AM REFUCKINGBORN.

The announcement of being "refuckingborn" didn't just apply to @MayorEmanuel himself, but to my approach to writing the character as well. Gone was the need to compress actions into a couple of Tweets, stories into self-contained units, and actions into the world we lived in. Even the profanity began to transform from the creative word combinations of the early days to much more utilitarian and pragmatic curses. Interestingly, that series of candy-corn Tweets also introduced the idea of multiple dimensions ("I can see through motherfucking time") and the importance of celery salt to the story—not only is it the crucial ingredient in the Chicago-style hot dog, it is also a sacrament delivered by Daley to Emanuel at the end of the story.

From that point on, @MayorEmanuel's world continued to diverge from our own in ways small and large. But perhaps nothing diverged as much as the week in January that saw Rahm Emanuel removed from the ballot, and saw @MayorEmanuel take up temporary residence under a bridge, befriend a duck, and set out on an ice floe down the Chicago River.

The funny thing about that storyline was that it shouldn't have happened. I should have been at work the day Emanuel was kicked off the ballot, but was home instead with an incredibly painful tooth abscess. As a result, I was online when the news was announced that Emanuel was off the ballot, and I was able to post within minutes:

Motherfucking shit fucking fuck shitters. What the fucking fuck motherfucking happened?!

The subsequent trashing of the apartment was easy: fury came naturally when writing @MayorEmanuel. But the next day was a lot harder. Finding a voice for the character when he wasn't angry—when he was exhausted from the fight and despondent about his chances—was more difficult. The story got quiet, the actions slower. He feeds a duck, he rides on the ice. The language changed, the pacing was different:

Woke up to Hambone licking my face. Now we're tossing chunks of ice into the river. Big fucking splash. Scared the ducks.

The river water is brown like coffee, but it sure doesn't taste like coffee. I think I miss coffee the motherfucking most.

There's a duck along the river here who has a bill with a little dark spot on it, like a mustache. Named him Quaxelrod. Quack fucking quack.

Me, Hambone and Quaxelrod found a pretty sturdy sheet of ice and we're going to fucking float down the river for a while.

Finding tone in 140-character bursts continued to be a challenge throughout the feed, but a welcome one. It was one that eventually equaled the importance of reacting to news as it broke.

Breaking News, Broken News

As the audience for the account grew—Emanuel getting kicked off the ballot brought 8,000 new followers in a single day—so too did speculation on who the author might be. One of the "tells" that many pointed to in trying to figure out who the author was was the accuracy with which @MayorEmanuel would track to campaign appearances or to breaking news.

"If you read those Tweets, there is an almost real-time knowledge of Rahm's schedule or ongoing events," Cook County Commissioner John Fritchey told the *Chicago Tribune* in a February 2 story about the account. "I think that's telling in and of itself."

Because of this fact, speculation often pointed to someone on the campaign trail or perhaps inside the Emanuel campaign itself. This always astounded me: the guy was the leading candidate for mayor of Chicago, not someone forming a secret society. His appearances were well publicized in the news, on the web and, yes, on Twitter itself. Really, knowing what Emanuel was doing wasn't that hard—you just had to listen.

It helped that I'd programmed a great tool for listening, the Chicago Mayoral Scorecard. It was a serious project, independent of @MayorEmanuel, that collected the latest news about and social media presence of the candidates for the election and published it all to the web, in real time. It also tracked poll numbers and campaign finance information, including the mapping of every donation to a candidate. It offered a unique view into the race and became a popular tool for people following the election. How it was that nobody connected the dots from the Scorecard to @MayorEmanuel still surprises me to this day. The Scorecard garnered some modest local press, and was watched closely by many local media types and politicians (including multiple mayoral candidates).

What the Scorecard allowed in terms of @MayorEmanuel was a single stop for collecting news on every candidate, as well as a quick heads-up on his or her recent Twitter updates. It was incredibly helpful, though it didn't replace monitoring Twitter, Facebook, and the news personally as well.

Near the end of the campaign, the Emanuel campaign pulled off a stunt where Rahm visited every ward in Chicago over two days: they called it 50 Wards in 50 Hours, and updated Twitter with each stop. This one was tricky: Emanuel's social media team was never very good at updating in real time, but they did a great job with this. In order to keep up (I was actually quite busy that day with a consulting job), I set Emanuel's real Twitter account to text my phone whenever it updated— allowing me to concentrate on my work, and hit the beats as they did.

Twitter was also an incredible tool for figuring out where candidates were. Even when they themselves weren't sending out Tweets, someone else usually was, so I kept a persistent Twitter search running on every candidate's name. This was especially helpful for L station spottings, appearances at lunch places, and other, more spontaneous, appearances.

For the orchestrated media events, the local media dutifully reported and tweeted the candidates' every moves. Honestly, it was almost too easy to figure it out.

The Hunter Games

As the speed and frequency of the updates increased, so too did the speculation around who was writing the account. It was a question that, as the election dragged on, the media became more interested in answering.

"Speculating about who is behind @MayorEmanuel is a popular parlor game among Chicago political types," *Politico*'s Molly Ball wrote on January 26, 2011. "Most believe it is a local, possibly a member of Chicago's famed Second City comedy troupe."

The *Chicago Tribune* went so far as to write a quasi-psychological profile:

> The references to Kanye West, Jeff Tweedy (a Rahm supporter), "Say Anything" and Guns N' Roses, among others, suggest someone culturally engaged and 40ish. Reference to the Tribune Tower and the newspaper itself, including blow-by-blow Tweets from a mayoral candidates' meeting with the editorial board, suggest someone clued in journalistically.

Honestly, they weren't very far off—though they aged me by a few years. Privately, a number of local reporters have now told me that I was on their short list for possible culprits, but very few people publicly named me as a suspect. It did happen though, and each time was based on the fact that I was a very early follower of the @MayorEmanuel account (though not the first, I was careful about that).

The problem was, being an early follower of a popular account wasn't enough proof—it was just a sign that I could spot a web trend before others. And, as a result, I would respond with a simple "Ha ha, I wish," and by and large that would be enough. Nobody seemed to dig very deeply—doing so would have unraveled the mystery pretty quickly. An astute reader could have noted similarities in voice, in the services used to update the account (for about half the campaign I was using a very esoteric Android Twitter client, Seesmic, for both my personal account and for @MayorEmanuel. This last was a clue that nobody picked up on until after I'd stopped using Seesmic for my own Twitter account). Another clue was the people regularly @replied to (friends of mine may have been slightly more likely to receive a response from @MayorEmanuel, though I tried to obfuscate that).

Another tell, which my wife was convinced was going to be the giveaway, was less about what was there than what *wasn't* there: I had only ever retweeted @MayorEmanuel once, the third Tweet on the first day. After that, I never mentioned the feed on my own Twitter account, never retweeted it, and never responded to those who did. The cone of silence that surrounded my personal account and @MayorEmanuel was a major giveaway, if someone had looked for it. But nobody was really looking that hard. At least, not yet.

The Bounty

That changed significantly on February 15, 2011, when, a week before Election Day, Rahm Emanuel called into the *Roe Conn Show*, a popular Chicago afternoon drive-time radio show. Emanuel was a day into his 50 Wards/50 Hours tour, but took time to phone in to the show's "super celebrity hotline."

The conversation that followed was a typical campaign Q&A: his tour of the wards, taxes and pensions, unions, and more. But at the 15-minute mark, it took a turn for the surreal:

"I have to ask you really fast about this, Rahm," Roe Conn said. "You have a lot of followers on Twitter, including myself, but that guy that's out there as the fake Rahm Emanuel has 21,000 followers on Twitter. What do you think about that guy?"

It was a question Emanuel had been asked before. But his answer this time was decidedly different:

> Here's what I'm gonna do, after the election; I am offering a donation to the charity of that gentleman's or woman's choice, if they would come forward and identify themselves . . . I will offer a $2,500 or $5,000 personal contribution to the charity of that individual's choice if they were to make public who they are.

The @MayorEmanuel @reply stream lit up immediately—mostly with people saying "It's a trap!"—and the Internet followed soon after, with dozens of blogs and news sites covering Emanuel's offer: "Emanuel Puts Bounty on His Twitter Imposter," "Rahm Emanuel Offers Bounty for Fake Twitter Feed," "Rahm Emanuel offers Twitter bounty."

Notice that something's misleading about those headlines: There was no bounty—it was an offer to make a charitable donation to a charity that the author designated. But accuracy isn't often done well online and so a bounty it was.

The problem, for me, was that there was a pretty big difference between hiding from a handful of curious reporters and hiding from posses looking to collect from Rahm Emanuel. And so what was already a growing sense of being hunted bloomed into full-fledged paranoia. My train rides—still the main place the stories were written—became fraught with the feeling of being watched. I started accessing the web version of Twitter exclusively through Google Chrome's Incognito Window, which doesn't keep a history of visits. I did everything I could to stay hidden, because I knew something that nobody else did: The story was coming to a close. And I didn't want to ruin the ending.

Waiting for the End of the World

What started as a lark eventually turned into something intentional, but that intention had a beginning, a middle, and, most important, an end. The story of @MayorEmanuel was always the story of the election.

Things end, nothing lasts forever. That's something that I've always believed, and something that @MayorEmanuel told David Axelrod on their last day together:

> **"There must be something we can do . . ." But there's not. Only things that fucking suck never end: look at laundry, or dishes.**

It's a sentiment that I shared with the *AV Club* years earlier, when *Punk Planet*, the magazine I had run for 13 years, came to a close: "Eras end, you know? It's horrendously sad, and I wish it didn't have to end with us, but things come to a close. Chapters are supposed to end."

The election was a week away, on February 22. This story needed to end.

The setup to the end had been a long time coming. Very little of the story was planned in advance—much of the writing was pure freestyle—and in some ways, the end was no different. But in others, it was. As the depth of my writing increased, I started to get little moments, images, and emotional beats in my head—things that would eventually take shape as a fully formed story or just as a concept that would be visited later in a single Tweet.

One of the earliest examples of this was an idea I had back in December: at some point close to the end of the campaign, Emanuel would meet Mayor Daley on the green roof of City Hall and have a conversation about the job of the mayor. At the time, the conversation was going to be about what a rough job it is, about how everyone ends up hating you in the end. But I gave a version of that speech from Daley, when he met up with a despondent @MayorEmanuel floating down the Chicago River on an ice floe:

> "Here's something my dad told me once: The role of the mayor is to be the guy that everyone takes a shit on. And then to shit on them back."

> "Except he didn't say 'everyone'; he said, 'Blacks, Jews, Poles, and Hippies,' but those were different times. Fucking substance is the same."

At the same time, I'd been sowing the seeds of a multiverse since the morning @MayorEmanuel visited Google Chicago. That day the *New York Times* had run a story about the account and I thought that the idea of a fake account becoming sentient—understanding that it's not the original person—was a great way to move far outside the boundaries of traditional parody.

Those two ideas began to come together the week before the election, when @MayorEmanuel ate fermented babyfood and went on a daylong hallucination. The hide-and-seek game that preceded the trip was a direct response to Emanuel's on-air offer to the author of the account, and throughout the day the characters he met (dead Chicagoans, all) warned him that "he's looking for you." The "he" in that sentence changed during the course of the day: At first, I considered it to be a direct retort to the radio appearance: Emanuel was looking for me. But then I decided that it was more ambiguous: *Someone* was looking for @MayorEmanuel. And there was something else as well:

And I'm flying backwards fucking fast, but I hear Curtis yell out "NOTHING IS WHAT IT SEEMS, MAN. WHAT IF YOU'RE NOT YOU?"

A few days later, that someone revealed himself: Mayor Daley. It was the logical answer to the combining of the two endgames I'd envisioned: Mayor Daley reveals the multiverse. All the rest was just detail: the kidnapping, the celery salt, the big BBQ grill. Most of that had actually come together the day before, while I was out on a walk with my wife and son—I remember telling her, and she looked at me like I was crazy (I'd seen that look before). But there it was: an end.

End Hits

The series of Tweets on the roof of City Hall on February 21 clearly set up the chess pieces for the end game: Only one Mayor Emanuel would survive the election. The only problem really was which election? February 22 was the first possibility—if Emanuel captured 50% + 1 vote, he would be elected Mayor of Chicago. However, if he fell below that threshold, he and the next closest competitor would be matched in a runoff election on April 5.

The election wasn't even close: Emanuel won 55% of the vote; Gery Chico the runner-up, commanded only 24% (Del Valle had 9.3%, Braun 9%, Van Pelt Watkins 1.6%, and Walls .9%). It was a commanding victory, and one I almost missed—everyone was predicting a long night, so I had taken my time eating dinner with my family. Everyone was wrong: the election was called by CNN less than an hour after the polls closed.

I was really caught off-guard—a big part of me (besides the fact that I'd written myself into a corner) thought there would be a runoff. And suddenly, the election was over. Which meant that the account was soon to follow. I knew the end of the account meant that it was all low notes the next day, so the election night account ended on a high one:

This party's going to go all fucking night. Fuck you, tomorrow, you're just gonna have to wait.

. . .

The morning didn't wait long, and with it came two things:

1) The last Tweet about coffee from @MayorEmanuel, "Motherfucking coffee, I'm going to drink you like there's no goddamn tomorrow."
2) An editorial from the *Chicago Tribune* editorial board urging the account to "@keepitgoing" (that really should have been a hashtag, not an @, but so it goes):

> We were alarmed when some followers suggested that a series of foreboding election-eve Tweets might signal the Twitter narrative is coming to an end. Perhaps @MayorEmanuel's work is done; perhaps he (or she) ran out of things to say or, you know, got a job. . . . @MayorEmanuel, if you're listening: Please don't. The fun is just beginning, and the mystery is almost as delicious as the Tweets themselves.

But it wasn't to be. The end was already there.

The final Tweets are some of my favorites, in that they demonstrate just how far the account had come in terms of language, tone, and efficiency. Like this one, where the whole day is encapsulated in a single Tweet:

And we sit down and plan out one last, perfect, day: lunch at Manny's, mooning Chico, tossing fucking bread to Quaxelrod.

And each one of those events is given just a single Tweet as well:

Watching Axelrod eat at Manny's is like watching Da Vinci paint the motherfucking Mona Lisa: a work of art.

Driving around in Axelrod's Civic, doing loops around the block outside Chico's offices, my ass hanging out of the missing window, laughing.

Tossing bread to Quaxelrod under the Cortland Street Bridge. The view from here is motherfucking incredible.

A reader that day postulated that the author of @MayorEmanuel had lost heart—the minimalism and quiet that had taken over the account was a marked difference from the raucous celebration of the day before. But it was intentional—the same kind of intention that plays out those very same Tweets in this book without annotation. Even for an account that had its volume set to 11 most times, quiet is good, sometimes.

The original plan was to have @MayorEmanuel, Axelrod, Carl the Intern, Hambone, and Quaxelrod drive to City Hall, return to the roof, and descend into the time vortex that way. But that evening, having dinner with my wife and son, the sky opened up above Chicago. When that late-February hailstorm hit, I knew there wasn't any time. I actually stood up from dinner, said "I have to finish this," and went about crafting the final Tweets of the @MayorEmanuel story.

And then the sky fucking opens up on us, and there's chunks of ice flying down. And it's pretty clear that the party's over.

I didn't know exactly how it was going to end. The only image I had in my head was giving a chance for Carl the Intern to tell @MayorEmanuel that he loved him, and for @MayorEmanuel to respond the same way Han Solo did in *The Empire Strikes Back*—the last cultural reference of the story:

Carl the Intern can't even make eye contact, but he's reaching out, and I touch his hand. And he says, "I love you," and I say, "I know."

Beyond that, it was entirely improvised. Axelrod reciting the Kaddish, the Jewish mourning prayer, came from a reader in an @reply, who'd said he was reciting the Kaddish as the end of the story unfolded. The final scene with the two animals also came from readers who wanted to know if Hambone and Quaxelrod were there. During the course of that 140 characters, @MayorEmanuel disappeared:

Quaxelrod flies over, and dips his little head, touching my fading shoe. Hambone just curls softly between my invisible legs.

And then came the last two Tweets: images and words from the beyond:

I can see a thousand fucking skylines, and they are all as motherfucking glorious as the first, and I can feel the touch of my friends.

And now all I can hear is that music, and suddenly everything just fucking . . .

The thought cuts off, the vortex closed. I had a final, single word keyed into my Tweet box for a few minutes, but I stopped myself from posting it. I still know what it is, of course. But it's mine.

II

The Courtship of @MayorEmanuel

"You are obviously a genius fake twitterer. Can we talk? We'd love to do a piece on/with you in @TheAtlantic."

It was Election Day morning, and Alexis Madrigal, a writer for *The Atlantic*, was trying to get @MayorEmanuel to contact him. It was something reporters did frequently, and shooting them down had become a sport.

When Molly Ball from *Politico* wrote on January 26, she asked, "I write for *Politico* and I'd like to talk to you. What are the chances?"

@MayorEmanuel's response: "Somewhere right between fucking slim and fucking none."

That was a polite brush-off comparatively. Most reporters got responses like "Sure, just give me a call: (312) E-A-T-S-H-I-T" or "Plouffe handles most of my press. Give him a call: (202) F-U-C-K-O-F-F."

Madrigal knew what he was getting into: "I'd seen what he had done to other reporters," he later told the *American Journalism Review*, "which was essentially mock them mercilessly." But because it was Election Day and I was busy with work, I ignored Madrigal, figuring he'd just go away. He didn't. Forty minutes later, he posted again:

"I think it is incumbent on you to at least tell me to fuck off." He included his e-mail, in a public-facing Tweet—that got my attention. But still, @MayorEmanuel responded:

I have a motherfucking election to win, and possibly a time vortex to dissolve into. You think I have fucking time to reply?

Which, of course, was not a *no*. And Madrigal seemed to pick up on that fact:

Everyone has 15 minutes, I hear. Maybe you can just send me your time vortex suicide note?

There was no suicide note. Instead, from the same anonymous e-mail account I had used to set up the account in the first place, I sent an e-mail to Madrigal:

OK, asshole
1) You tweet about this and it's over before it even begins.
2) You're a journalist, pitch me.

That was all it said. It had begun.

Killing the Ponies

From that e-mail spun 48 hours of back-and-forth between Madrigal and myself. I kept him in the dark about who he was communicating with, and tried to keep him guessing whether he had the story or not.

Some of that was because it was fun to watch him sweat (many of the early e-mails from him are punctuated with questions like, "5 hours til the polls close . . . Are we getting somewhere? What can we do?"), but it was also because I was deeply conflicted about whether I wanted to reveal myself or not.

I tried to string Madrigal along as I worked out in my head what it was I actually wanted. Part of what I wanted was to see if he was the right guy for the story. And that meant testing him with lines like "the *New York Times* is promising all the piggyback rides I want. Plus a pony." His response to that one was the first time that I thought he might work out:

"Damn! Now I have to kill everyone at the *New York Times*. And every pony."

Election day continued that way, with a running back-and-forth about the various absurd goods that were waiting for me, if I revealed my identity:

Madrigal: You know we have a zipline from our offices here at The Watergate to Pelosi's apartment, right? Use of it comes with a bottle of bourbon and diplomatic passport.

Me: Why would you use a zipline? You know about the tunnel, right?

Madrigal: There's nothing quite like crashing through a plate glass window.

It was fun, and it convinced me that he got it. But I was still uneasy about everything, a fact that I laid bare for him the next day:

I'm going to drop the pretension and just be honest with you: I am wildly ambivalent about "coming out" on this. Not because I'm worried about Rahm or anything like that, but because I know that it's going to make my life temporarily very crazy. The *Chicago Tribune* ran an editorial today pleading with @ ME to keep going. These things were not intentional, by any stretch of the fucking imagination.

Anyway, this is just a way of saying yes/no/maybe/jesus.

Madrigal responded with a lengthy e-mail, the tone completely different from the jokes and barbs the day before. An excerpt:

To me, your ambivalence is (a very good) part of the story. The jester can't show up in jeans and a t-shirt and sling the same jokes at the king. I don't know how much of a literature nerd you are, but Twitter sometimes gets me thinking about the Russian theorist Bakhtin's ideas about the carnivalesque. In the carnival, the distance between the powerful and others shrinks and at times the relationship even flips. Everyone tends to wear a mask, though, because it's a temporary state and you know eventually the normal will snap back into place.

But, whatever else happens, you've done a real public service and struck that *Daily Show* chord: We want our politics to be more real than it is, and when it's not, we want someone to call it out liberally spiked with motherfuckers. You've created what Kundera called the devil's laughter, the kind that recognizes the absurd and makes the heavy light.

I responded with a single line e-mail: "Yeah, you'll do."

The Story Hits

Alexis Madrigal's story went live on *The Atlantic*'s website at 1:15 on Monday, February 28, 2011. It had been five days since the @MayorEmanuel account went dormant, and I thought that maybe things had calmed down from the highs of the week before, which had seen @MayorEmanuel make appearances in every major news organization in the States (and some around the world).

I'd arranged with Madrigal that the story would break on a Monday specifically because I didn't teach again until Wednesday and I thought that two days might be enough for the news to blow over. I couldn't have been more wrong.

From the moment *The Atlantic* went live with the story, my personal Twitter account exploded, my e-mail inbox filled, and friend requests on Facebook began to pile up. Instantly. I talk about the power of the real-time web a lot. But I had never really witnessed it firsthand until then.

In an instant, the secret that had been held so closely—known only by my wife and four friends (made closer by this experience)—was public. And I didn't know what to expect.

In an earlier communication with Madrigal I expressed it this way:

> I don't know if it's reluctance—obviously, I wrote you. It's hesitancy. A realization that things are going to possibly, maybe, spin out of control for a while. And not wanting that—or not knowing if I want that. Maybe it's not reluctance. Maybe it's wanting to extend that quiet moment with a duck on the river, before you toss yourself into a vortex of your own making.

Before the news broke, I'd left town for the weekend, trying to extend that moment of quiet out as much as possible (in a reversal of the Wisconsin Senate exodus, my wife, son, and I escaped *to* Wisconsin, holing up in a hotel in Milwaukee). But it was over now.

An hour and forty-five minutes after *The Atlantic* story broke, my doorbell rang. I had been sitting on the couch in my living room, my back to the front window. I turned around and saw a news van parked outside. I dove off the couch and crawled across the floor to the bedroom. My wife, who had come home early as she saw the news spread across the web, ran in after me.

We held a quick, panicked discussion in the bedroom, peering through the drapes as the newsman continued to ring the bell. They weren't going away. *Shit.*

Reluctantly, I opened the door. "Did you really have to come to my house?" I asked the three men standing in front of me, one in a suit and overcoat, one carrying a camera.

The guy in the suit introduced himself. He was Ben Bradley from Channel 7, the ABC affiliate in Chicago. I actually recognized his name from the @MayorEmanuel @reply stream: he was a fan. At least there was that.

They came to my house only after going to my work, he explained—which was by no means a consolation. And, he added, while they were here now, "everyone else" would be here soon. *Great.* And then he uttered a phrase that I never need to hear again:

"There are two ways we can do this."

Two ways. Either I could let him and his news team in, they'd take ten minutes to shoot an interview, and then they'd go—and the other news teams would do the same—or I could close the door and they'd do the story anyway, but talk with my neighbors, coworkers, and "your parents in Glenview" (a detail I hadn't offered up).

There wasn't much I could do at that point. Disturbing my neighbors and colleagues didn't sound like a good decision, though my parents were out of town, so they'd be safe (though when they came back, they had messages on their voice mail from TV crews and reporters). I told them I'd do the interview, but they'd have to wait outside.

My wife and I furiously cleaned the living room, I removed any pictures of our son from the room, we closed any other door in the house, and we invited them in.

The Two Mayors (redux)

The question that was asked repeatedly that day—from the reporters who came to my house (three other news crews would eventually arrive; only the CBS affiliate was missing), from the journalists who called, and the thousands of people on e-mail, Facebook, and Twitter—was what about Rahm's $5,000?

Oh right. *That.* I was still ambivalent about collecting—I knew that by doing so, I was at risk of being co-opted, something I was decidedly uninterested in.

What I didn't know was that the $5,000 had actually become $10,000—a fund-raising startup named Causes.com had offered to match Emanuel's donation. That news was delivered the next day in an e-mail from Roe Conn, cohost of the *Roe & Roeper* show on WLS, where Emanuel had first made the charity offer two weeks before. I was stunned. That was real money for an organization. There was no way I was leaving it on the table.

The deal was that the check from Emanuel would be presented live on the air at the WLS studios on Wednesday May 2. I decided not to reveal who the recipient would be in advance—I've always fantasized about the idea of just suddenly getting a pile of money out of nowhere, and I thought it would be cool to be the person who could grant that to someone else.

In my mind this was going to be easy: a radio appearance, Rahm and me, and the two hosts. That's it—15 minutes in and out, and a great cause would get a nice check at the end of it.

Not so fast.

At 4 pm, a producer for the show e-mailed me the press release they had just issued:

> Chicago, IL—Mayor-elect Rahm Emanuel will present a $5,000 check to Twitter impersonator Dan Sinker (@MayorEmanuel) on WLS-AM's Roe Conn Show with Richard Roeper on Wednesday, March 2 at 5 p.m.

It was an invite to the press. This wasn't going to be what I'd thought.

■ ■ ■

The next day, as I walked down State Street toward the radio studio, I was recognized by a homeless person outside the Harold Washington Library: *You're the guy from the newspaper,* he called. And I was; my mug had filled the cover of the *Chicago Tribune* the day before.

As I approached WLS from the south, a TV crew waiting out front called, "Here he comes!" as I walked up. Once inside, Ben Bradley—the same reporter who had been on my front stoop two days before—hopped in the elevator with me.

"Who's up there?" I asked him.

"Everyone," he replied.

Great.

The elevator doors opened and I was ushered into a waiting room—a waiting room with no door. Press swooped in and I realized that I was in for far more than I'd bargained for.

I don't know how long I was in that doorless room. Long enough for some very awkward video of me, sweating and nervous, to exist on the Internet forever, I suppose.

They kept Emanuel and me separated, like lovers on their wedding day. Presumably his waiting room had a door.

Finally, they led me into the studio and I was blinded by a wall of cameras and floodlights.

Holy shit.

We were in a tiny room—it had to have been 10×15 or so. There was a large table in the middle, set up with four mics, two on each side. The hosts, Richard Roeper and Roe Conn, were standing with their backs to the bank of cameras, while two open mics on the opposite side of the table waited for Emanuel and me.

I took my place at the mic, squinted into the glare of the camera lights, and managed to stammer out a few things. But mostly I just turned an increasingly dark shade of red and stood there.

Emanuel was brought in a few moments later, a stark contrast to me in every way: calm, collected, and surprisingly tiny.

"Relax, man," he said as we shook hands.

"I am *so* not relaxed," I responded.

The meeting was jocular and brief. Listen to the audio and you can hear a near-constant stream of cameras clicking in the background. I was not at my most eloquent, stammering my way through the few sentences I was given time to utter. I was so far out of my element I might as well have been on the moon.

Standing in that tiny room, cameras rolling, I realized that a politician's gift is perhaps simply the ability to stay calm when the spotlight is on. While I had buckets of flop sweat dripping off me,

Rahm stood there as if standing in a room stuffed with camera people was the most natural experience in the world.

He handed me a check for $5,000 made out to Young Chicago Authors, the high-school writing program I had chosen. Years ago, they had featured me in *Say What*, a student-made magazine the organization published. That put them on my radar, and I followed what they were doing over the years that followed, always in awe. The next day I would give the check to people from YCA, who were at the college where I taught, for their Louder Than a Bomb poetry slam finals. We'd stand together in my office, no cameras, no anything. It was better.

Rahm had clearly rehearsed, and the talking points rolled off his tongue easily. He was reassuring ("You have tenure, man; don't worry, I already called about it"), sharp-witted, and a surprisingly good sport. He talked a lot about after-school programs and the importance of education. My choice of YCA gave him latitude to portray six months of profanity as something productive: "What he's doing—this *impersonator*—is something serious and gives kids an outlet to find their voice . . . So I want to support what he's doing with our kids."

It wasn't until a day later, when the local press attention on @MayorEmanuel had shifted entirely to Young Chicago Authors and Louder Than a Bomb that I realized what Emanuel had done: he had engineered an outcome where everyone won.

This was a guy who could have destroyed me. Not in the *ha-ha, you're at the bottom of the Chicago River* kind of way. But had he reacted differently—had he said that he wanted the person to stop, that it was disrespectful, that it was *dangerous*—the outcome would have been very different. I'd probably be out of a job. The book you're holding would probably not exist.

During the radio interview, Emanuel said that he first found out about the account because "a number of people e-mailed or called and said, '*What are you doing?*'"

Instead of requesting that Twitter shut the account down—which, in the early days, could have been done without raising a single hackle—or coming out strongly against it, some kind of bizarre mental calculus was performed and Emanuel and his team decided to chuckle along with everyone else. "There are many times," he told the *Roe & Roeper* show, "where I said, *My sentiments exactly.*"

III

The Meme's the Thing

Within moments of President Obama's announcement that Osama bin Laden had been killed, @OsamaInHell made his Twitter debut, tweeting "Wait, what?" The anonymous account has kept tweeting every day since, painting a hilarious portrait of the banalities of the afterlife ("The water here tastes like Advil after the candy coating melts off"), and offering his take on life on the surface ("Every time Obama says 'democracy' we have to take a shot of santorum").

When the *Deepwater Horizon* drilling platform exploded in the Gulf of Mexico on April 20, 2010, it sent 4.9 million barrels of oil streaming up from the deep over the next three months. BP, the company responsible for the spill, responded with public statements that were derided in *Newsweek* as ranging "from awkward to awful, causing offense all over again with inappropriate statements and tone-deaf tweets." The sharpest response to BP came from Twitter in the form of @BPGlobalPR, which, a month after the spill began, tweeted, "We regretfully admit that something has happened off of the Gulf Coast. More to come." and proceeded to rip into the company with biting humor through the duration of the spill.

The very same day that Sarah Palin was announced as John McCain's running mate for the 2008 presidential election, @Fake SarahPalin tweeted: "Fact: I'm little known." For almost three years now, the account has continued to parody the former governor of Alaska, commenting on the swine flu panic ("THERE IS NO SUCH THING AS PIG FLU. THEY DONT EVEN HAVE CHIMNEYS. AL GORE HAS TRICKED YOU AGAIN!!"), her family ("Willow Palin, WHY DOES YOUR BREATH SMELL LIKE CAT FOOD?"), and her presidential ambitions for 2012 ("So basically to become president, all I have to do is beat Mitt "Obamacare" Romney and Tim Pawlenty? THAT. IS. HILARIOUS").

This is the landscape we live in today: If you're a public figure or even a public phenomenon (there were dozens of Rapture-related parody accounts set up in the lead-up to that nonevent), the chances that a doppelgänger, or two, exists on Twitter, or that a mocking "fan" page has been set up on Facebook, are pretty high.

Hell, there was both a @DanSinkersBeard and a @ProfessorSinker account set up within a day or so of my sudden notoriety. You roll with it.

When photos from inside the White House Situation Room appeared on the web, they were Photoshopped almost immediately. As Alexis Madrigal (the guy's inescapable) wrote in *The Atlantic*, "It was only a matter of time before the photoshoppers went to work on the iconic image, using it as grist for the always-grinding humor mill of the Internet. Already, Keanu Reeves, the grumpy flower girl, a Velociraptor, and the shocked cat have been edited into the photo. The Situation Room has been colonized. It is part of our world."

In fact, that "colonization" of the Situation Room photos played a part in the administration's decision not to release Osama bin Laden's death photos. As ABC's Jake Tapper reported on May 12, 2011, in a piece titled "Gates: Not Releasing OBL Corpse Photos Was 'the Right Decision'—Especially in Light of the Photoshopped Situation Room Photos." Defense Secretary Robert Gates explained to Tapper, "We were also worried about the potential for manipulation of those photos and doing things with those photos that would be pretty outrageous in terms of provoking a reaction that might in fact put our troops at greater risk in both Iraq and Afghanistan."

Welcome to today, where photos of a dead terrorist leader might appear alongside LOLcats and dancing babies. A brave new world indeed.

The Quick and the Dead

But is this world so different from the one that came before? After all, *Saturday Night Live* has been lampooning the news of the week since the 1970s. That's the same time frame in which Garry Trudeau has been skewering politicians in the comic strip *Doonesbury*, which famously portrayed George W. Bush as a floating asterisk in a Roman helmet. Berkeley Breathed took an even more surrealistic approach to political satire in the 1980s comic strip *Bloom County*. And caricature itself—the idea of exaggerating the prominent features of a person—was practiced by Leonardo da Vinci himself. So, is a world that doesn't take its politicians or its politics all that seriously so different from the one that we lived in before?

No, not at all—we've been making each other laugh by mocking the world around us for millennia—the Greeks' "old comedy" taunted both political figures and religion. Nothing's new in that respect—we just see new forms of it emerge with new mediums. What *has* changed is the speed at which it can happen and the democratization of the tools available.

Doonesbury wouldn't have had the impact it did without the help of the newspaper industry Trudeau relied on for distribution—the same industry that allowed Mark Twain's satire to proliferate a hundred years before. *Saturday Night Live* is a multimillion-dollar production, produced by one of the big four broadcast channels. Hunter S. Thompson's gonzo journalism made its way into the acid-soaked culture of the '70s through the pages of *Rolling Stone*. Each work of satire required an expensive (and extensive) network of production and distribution to reach its audience. This wasn't something that you could easily just pick up and *do*—let alone have anyone see.

And yet that's the world we now live in: the tools are cheap (most of them are free), and the act of distributing your work is as simple as a click. Video, audio, photos, animation, and of course text, instantly available to anyone with an Internet connection—do not pass go, do not collect $200. It certainly doesn't mean it's all good and it doesn't mean that it will be seen. But it means it has a chance. Which is more than it had back when there were gatekeepers at every door.

We see it every day now, with satire, with humor, with funny cat videos, and with things that are far, far more serious. The "Arab Spring" uprisings and revolutions in Tunisia and Egypt were aided by information posted and spread on Facebook and Twitter. Word from Japan following the earthquake and tsunami there reached US shores far more readily on Twitter, YouTube, and Flickr than via the news organizations that needed to get reporters on flights before they could have live shots. The Osama bin Laden news has been referred to as "Twitter's CNN moment," but it's just one of many times that the service has proven to be an information lifeline for those connected to it.

When *New York Times* reporter Brian Stelter reached tornado-devastated Joplin, Missouri, on May 23, 2011, he discovered that the communication infrastructure had been destroyed. In a blog post on May 27, he wrote:

> It's easy to scoff at the suggestion that satisfactory cell service is a matter of national security and necessity. But I won't scoff anymore. If I were planning a newsroom's response to emergencies, I would buy those backpacks that have six or eight wireless cards in them, all connected to different cell tower operators, thereby upping the chances of finding a signal at any given time.

The most effective method that Stelter found for updating both his newsroom and his audience was Twitter. He was able to post to it via SMS texts, with most eventually going through on the crippled cell towers of Joplin.

> I started trying to tweet everything I saw—the search of the rubble pile, the sounds coming from the hospital, the dazed look on people's faces.

> Some of the texts didn't send, but most did. Practically speaking, text messages were my only way to relay information. I tried to make phone calls to the desk in New York, but the calls always dropped within a minute. I tried to send e-mails, but they sat in my outbox.

Twitter, because it scales all the way down to the simplest of communication mediums, the text message, became the only reliable tool at his disposal. A lot of people dismiss the service because of its "arbitrary" 140-character limit, but it's there for a reason: Text messages cap at 160 characters, and they needed 20 characters for the namespace. Allowing unfettered access to Twitter via SMS means that the cheapest phones on the simplest plans can communicate to a potential audience of 200 million.

It is the understatement of the year to say that the scale of information on the Internet is enormous. A single statistic from a single site—48 hours' worth of video is uploaded to YouTube every minute—can make you feel like you've been dropped on your head. That scale creates staggering network effects, allowing information to spread at speeds that are almost impossible to fathom.

When rumors of Osama bin Laden's death began to spread on Twitter, its servers began to process Tweets at speeds they'd rarely seen before. By the time Obama appeared on TV and officially confirmed the raid on the bin Laden compound, Twitter was processing over 5,000 Tweets per second.

To put that in perspective, on average a hummingbird's wings beat about 25 times a second; Twitter was processing people's thoughts at a speed 200 times that of a hummingbird. The only time Twitter has moved faster was four seconds after midnight, January 1, 2011, in Japan, when the service processed 6,939 Tweets per second of people saying *akemashite omedetou gozaimasu*—Happy New Year.

The speed with which information can spread through services like Twitter is simply staggering, and unlike anything we've seen before. Whether it's best wishes for a new year, the news of a terrorist killed, or a satirical and surreal extended narrative of a historic mayoral election, Tweets pass through the network of Twitter with a freedom and speed unimaginable just a few years ago.

That speed is not just a technological marvel, however. It is a result of the participatory nature of the tool: Things don't spread on Twitter because Biz Stone, Evan Williams, and Jack Dorsey, the cofounders of the service, decide that they're important. They spread because the people you follow thought you should know. Enough people pass the information along the chain and suddenly you achieve unheard-of velocities—all because people cared enough to tell others about it. Among all the faceless technology—the servers and fiberoptics heaving under the weight of the messages that pass through them—there is something wonderfully human at the core.

Discovered (part two)

"Now why would you want to ruin all this fun?"

The response to my disingenuously flippant question popped into my in-box seven tense minutes later. My heart felt like it was going to rip through my chest and my hands shook as I reached for my keyboard. This could be it. It could be over.

"Look I'm impressed. I'm not going to ruin it," the e-mail began.

I felt dizzy—it was honestly hard to read, my heart and brain and breathing had gone all screwy.

"I love this city and its politics . . . I love what you're doing on both levels. I don't want to ruin it."

And he didn't. The guy who had figured out my identity would remain silent about his discovery for another five weeks. When Emanuel went on the radio and offered $5,000 for the author to come forward, he dropped another note:

"In case the money offer has you nervous, don't worry. My word is my bond."

Who was this guy? We exchanged e-mails back and forth. His name was Seth Lavin, and he was a 25-year-old Teach for America instructor in the Altgeld Gardens housing project, where he was teaching math to fifth graders. His wife was 41 weeks pregnant when news broke that a huge blizzard was going to hit Chicago, so he'd taken the day off to ensure that he'd be home in case his wife went into labor. That "meant I had an unexpected burst of sitting-around time," Lavin said. "I don't do well with sitting-around time." So he went about solving the mystery.

"I looked for an error in the beginning, before he became famous, before he was getting media attention," Lavin later told Chicago's WTTW after my identity had been revealed. "He had to have made a mistake."

The bit.ly links were that mistake. I'd actually shortened three links while logged in as @dansinker. Lavin was smart: he'd only shown me one. If I'd denied it, he still had two more in his pocket. Dozens of reporters, active Twitter users, and political operatives tried to figure out who @MayorEmanuel was—and none had thought to look at those three links. Thankfully.

I deleted the Tweets immediately—they were gone for good and appear in this book for the first time in their original context (minus the links though, because that would look weird)—and that was it, my tracks were covered. There was no other definitive proof that linked me to @MayorEmanuel.

When asked later why he didn't reveal my identity, Lavin told WTTW:

> There are two reasons. One is honor. I said to him, "I don't have any plans to out you but I can tell you how to cover your tracks' [and] I talk to my students about integrity and want them to live in an honorable world."

> The second reason: because it's fun. He's a modern Chicago folklorist. Someone who is capturing what the city is feeling when it doesn't even know it's feeling these things.

> Getting attention for finding him out was way less interesting than finding out how he was going to end the Twitter feed.

INDEX